THE
LONDON TRANSPORT
GOLDEN JUBILEE BOOK
1933-1983

First published by The Daily Telegraph 1983
Copyright © London Transport 1983

ISBNs (hardback) 0 901684 96 1
        (paperback) 0 901684 86 4

Published by The Daily Telegraph, 135 Fleet Street,
London EC4P 4BL
Designed, edited and produced by First Editions
(Rambletree Ltd)
Phototypeset by Oliver Burridge & Co. Ltd,
Crawley
Printed and bound in Great Britain by W. S. Cowell,
Ipswich

THE LONDON TRANSPORT
GOLDEN JUBILEE BOOK
1933-1983

OLIVER GREEN AND JOHN REED

The Daily Telegraph

Acknowledgements

The authors would like to thank the following for their valuable assistance in the preparation of this book:

Liz Richardson and Linda Browne for typing the manuscript; Robert Lansdown, Bert Holder, and Salim Mohamed for photographic work; Peter Wilson, Gill Cork and Sue Skelton of LT's Publicity Office, and many other colleagues in London Transport for information and advice.

Most of the photographs used in this book are from the London Transport Photographic Library, but some have been obtained from other sources:

Michael Beamish pages 124/125 (2), Birch (HJ Publications collection) 8/9 (3), Robert Bird 186/187 (4), H. C. Casserley 30/31 (Main pic), Leon Daniels (Obsolete Fleet Ltd) 34/35 (5), Michael Dryhurst 116/117 (1), Oliver Green 34/35 (4), 54/55 (4), 58/59 (3, 4 & 5), 94/95 (5), 102/103 (3), 138/139 (4), 142/143 (7), 162/163 (7), 168/169 (2), 170/171 (2), 178 (2), 188/189 (4), Imperial War Museum 78/79 (1), Fred Ivey 94/95 (4), 122/123 (1), 162/163 (8), Bruce Jenkins 114/115 (2 & 3), 122/123 (3 & 4), 126/127 (3 & 4), 162/163 (1–4), Barry Le Jeune 142/143 (1–3), 154/155 (3), B. R. Jones 130 (1), London Transport Museum 10/11 (1–4), 14/15 (1), 38/39 (3), 42/43 (4 & 5), 46/47 (1 & 2), 62 (2), 66/67 (1 & 2), 70/71 (2 & 3), 74/75 (2, 4 & 7), 82/83 (6), 86/87 (1), 88/89 (1–4, 7 & 8), 94/95 (2 & 6), 100/101 (1), 106/107 (1–4), 108/109 (3), 110/111 (3), 114/115 (1), 118/119 (1, 5 & 6), 150/151 (ticket), 180/181 (1), 184/185 (1–6), Collection of the late Prince Marshall 118/119 (4), 122/123 (5), Metro-Cammell Ltd 182/183 (1), Modern Transport 124/125 (1), John Reed 168/169 (3 & 4), 170/171 (Main pic and 1), 178 (3), 188/189 (5 & 6), John Topham Picture Library 118/119 (2), 130 (2), William Tucker 186/187 (2), W. J. Wyse 106/107 (3).

FOREWORD BY THE
CHAIRMAN OF LONDON TRANSPORT

The subject of public transport in any major city has an element of fascination for most people. Older generations will have fond memories of motor buses with open staircases, clanging tramcars and hissing trolleybuses—not just in London, of course, but in towns and cities all over Britain.

What surely makes London unique is the sheer size and complexity of its public transport system—or perhaps one should say 'systems', bearing in mind the intricate and complementary network of British Rail local services which lies beyond the scope of this book. London Transport carries over five million passengers every working day—a vital contribution to the mobility and life of London.

In 1983 we look back over fifty years of London Transport. The old London Passenger Transport Board, as it was originally called, inherited a motley collection of buses of many different types and colours, trams—some of them still open-top—a few trolleybuses and, of course, the Underground. The trams and trolleybuses are now just a memory, but we are, significantly perhaps, poised to enter the era of what some have termed the 'super-tram'—a new light railway which will link the City with Docklands and the Isle of Dogs. The Underground, too, is witnessing new developments: for example, the enormously successful extension of the Piccadilly Line into the heart of Heathrow Airport is all set to be projected into the proposed new Terminal 4. Equally important are the station modernisation programmes designed to update a system which had its beginnings in 1863.

The bus business, too, is looking ahead with trials about to start with BUSCO, a revolutionary new application of microchip technology to keep buses and controllers in close communication with each other. This will mean a big step forward in the struggle to maintain a regular service in London's choked traffic conditions.

So, while this book looks back over fifty years of progress and change, we in London Transport are actively involved in pursuing further developments needed to fit this great organisation for its role in moving London's millions in the decades ahead. The next fifty years will, I am sure, be no less exciting than the last.

KEITH BRIGHT

**55 BROADWAY, WESTMINSTER,
JANUARY 1983**

I
Moving Millions
1933-1939

BEEFIELD. FARNINGHAM   WALTER E. SPRADBERY

LONDON TRANSPORT

AT LONDON'S
SERVICE

(*Previous page*) A poster by Walter Spradbery, 1934.

July 1st 1933 was a warm, sunny day in London. Although it was a Saturday, many Londoners would have had to work that morning. In the afternoon, those with money and leisure had a wide choice of entertainments. They might bet on the horses at Alexandra Park, a popular north London racecourse which has since closed, or watch the Lawn Tennis Championships at Wimbledon, where the King and Queen could be glimpsed among the spectators. An excursion to Hampton Court offered the opportunity to view the handsome new bridge over the Thames due to be opened the following Monday by the Prince of Wales. That evening thousands of people would go to the cinema, either locally or in the West End, where Hollywood's latest triumph, *King Kong*, was showing at the Coliseum with '*no seats over 1/6d*'. Jessie Matthews, Gladys Cooper and Edith Evans could all be seen on the West End stage that night, and there was a last chance to catch the Crazy Gang in their final week of variety at the Holborn Empire.

Wherever Londoners went that day, as long as it was further than the shop on the corner, they were likely to go by bus, tram or tube. There was nothing outwardly different about their journeys on that summer Saturday, but as they read their morning papers, London's travellers learned that a silent transformation had taken place overnight. For the first time all of the capital's bus, tram and underground railway operations had been brought together under a single body. This newly created organisation was the London Passenger Transport Board, soon to be known simply as London Transport, and, according to one press report that morning, '*the largest traffic pool the world has ever known*'.

(1) The first London Passenger Transport Board at 55 Broadway, July 1933. The Chairman, Lord Ashfield, is seated centre. Frank Pick, Vice Chairman and Chief Executive, is standing second from the right.

(2) Not everyone welcomed the creation of London Transport, least of all the independent bus operators. Here three generations of the Birch family mourn the passing of their bus routes to the LPTB in 1934.

1

2

3

(3) Applying the new gold-lettered fleet name, a task which involved more than 12,000 road and rail vehicles, in May 1934.

As early as 1863, the year in which London's first underground line was opened, a committee report to the House of Lords had recommended that all the railways in the metropolis be put under one management. No progress whatsoever was made in this direction until the early 1900s when, largely out of commercial necessity, a series of mergers and takeovers by separate transport undertakings produced the Underground group of companies. By 1913 this large privately owned 'combine' included the main bus company (the London General), three tramway systems (the London United, Metropolitan Electric and South Metropolitan Electric) and all the underground railways except the short Waterloo & City line and the Metropolitan. The largest tramway network in the capital was run by the London County Council, while a number of boroughs in east and south London also ran their own municipal tramways. Finally, there were the overground suburban services of the main line railways, rationalised in 1923 into four large private companies.

During the 1920s traffic conditions in many parts of London deteriorated considerably. Some areas were inadequately served by the existing transport network, while others suffered from unproductive competition between different operators. The increasingly bitter conflict between the General and a variety of small 'pirate' independent bus companies was a particularly serious problem. Rival bus crews raced and blocked each other on the roads, and a number of accidents were caused by dangerous driving in the frantic battle for passengers. A series of reports by government advisory bodies suggested that the only solution to all these difficulties was to create a single authority responsible for all London's public transport.

In 1929 the Underground group and the LCC took the initiative by promoting two separate parliamentary bills to allow further coordination of their operations. A sudden change of government killed off both bills, but the Minister of Transport in the new Labour administration, Herbert Morrison, quickly came up with his own alternative proposals. Morrison recommended the creation of a new transport board for London to be run on similar lines to the recently established BBC and Central Electricity Board. It was to be self-supporting and unsubsidised, with a degree of public control but non-political management. The only major element of public transport in the capital excluded from the proposed authority was the overground suburban railway network. The four companies argued that their suburban services could not be run separately from their long distance passenger services, but they were prepared to consider the pooling of fare receipts and agreed to set up a joint committee with the new authority to plan future developments. No such compromise arrangement was offered to the independent bus operators, who remained firmly opposed to the scheme. Despite their active campaign against it, and a further change of government which re-

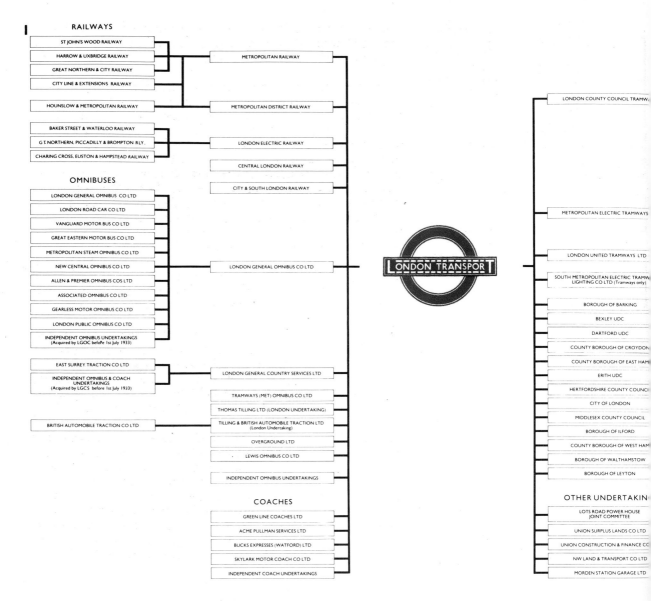

RAILWAYS

ST JOHN'S WOOD RAILWAY	
HARROW & UXBRIDGE RAILWAY	METROPOLITAN RAILWAY
GREAT NORTHERN & CITY RAILWAY	
CITY LINE & EXTENSIONS RAILWAY	
HOUNSLOW & METROPOLITAN RAILWAY	METROPOLITAN DISTRICT RAILWAY
BAKER STREET & WATERLOO RAILWAY	
G T. NORTHERN, PICCADILLY & BROMPTON RLY.	LONDON ELECTRIC RAILWAY
CHARING CROSS, EUSTON & HAMPSTEAD RAILWAY	
	CENTRAL LONDON RAILWAY
	CITY & SOUTH LONDON RAILWAY

OMNIBUSES

- LONDON GENERAL OMNIBUS CO LTD
- LONDON ROAD CAR CO LTD
- VANGUARD MOTOR BUS CO LTD
- GREAT EASTERN MOTOR BUS CO LTD
- METROPOLITAN STEAM OMNIBUS CO LTD
- NEW CENTRAL OMNIBUS CO LTD
- ALLEN & PREMIER OMNIBUS COS LTD
- ASSOCIATED OMNIBUS CO LTD
- GEARLESS MOTOR OMNIBUS CO LTD
- LONDON PUBLIC OMNIBUS CO LTD
- INDEPENDENT OMNIBUS UNDERTAKINGS (Acquired by LGOC before 1st July 1933)

LONDON GENERAL OMNIBUS CO LTD

- EAST SURREY TRACTION CO LTD
- INDEPENDENT OMNIBUS & COACH UNDERTAKINGS (Acquired by LGCS before 1st July 1933)

LONDON GENERAL COUNTRY SERVICES LTD

- BRITISH AUTOMOBILE TRACTION CO LTD

TRAMWAYS (MET) OMNIBUS CO LTD
THOMAS TILLING LTD (LONDON UNDERTAKING)
TILLING & BRITISH AUTOMOBILE TRACTION LTD (London Undertaking)
OVERGROUND LTD
LEWIS OMNIBUS CO LTD
INDEPENDENT OMNIBUS UNDERTAKINGS

COACHES

GREEN LINE COACHES LTD
ACME PULLMAN SERVICES LTD
BUCKS EXPRESSES (WATFORD) LTD
SKYLARK MOTOR COACH CO LTD
INDEPENDENT COACH UNDERTAKINGS

LONDON TRANSPORT

LONDON COUNTY COUNCIL TRAMW
METROPOLITAN ELECTRIC TRAMWAYS
LONDON UNITED TRAMWAYS LTD
SOUTH METROPOLITAN ELECTRIC TRAMW LIGHTING CO LTD (Tramways only)
BOROUGH OF BARKING
BEXLEY UDC
DARTFORD UDC
COUNTY BOROUGH OF CROYDON
COUNTY BOROUGH OF EAST HAM
ERITH UDC
HERTFORDSHIRE COUNTY COUNCIL
CITY OF LONDON
MIDDLESEX COUNTY COUNCIL
BOROUGH OF ILFORD
COUNTY BOROUGH OF WEST HAM
BOROUGH OF WALTHAMSTOW
BOROUGH OF LEYTON

OTHER UNDERTAKIN

LOTS ROAD POWER HOUSE JOINT COMMITTEE
UNION SURPLUS LANDS CO LTD
UNION CONSTRUCTION & FINANCE CO
NW LAND & TRANSPORT CO LTD
MORDEN STATION GARAGE LTD

(1) This chart shows the steady process of amalgamation leading to the eventual creation of London Transport in 1933.

The symbols of the three major transport undertakings taken over by the LPTB:

(2) The cap badge worn by bus crews of the London General Omnibus Company;

(3) The coat of arms of the London County Council carried by its tramcars after 1926;

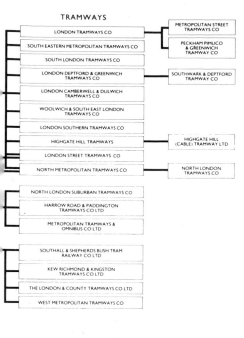

TRAMWAYS

- LONDON TRAMWAYS CO
- SOUTH EASTERN METROPOLITAN TRAMWAYS CO
- SOUTH LONDON TRAMWAYS CO
- LONDON DEPTFORD & GREENWICH TRAMWAYS CO
- LONDON CAMBERWELL & DULWICH TRAMWAYS CO
- WOOLWICH & SOUTH EAST LONDON TRAMWAYS CO
- LONDON SOUTHERN TRAMWAYS CO
- HIGHGATE HILL TRAMWAYS
- LONDON STREET TRAMWAYS CO
- NORTH METROPOLITAN TRAMWAYS CO

- METROPOLITAN STREET TRAMWAYS CO
- PECKHAM PIMLICO & GREENWICH TRAMWAY CO
- SOUTHWARK & DEPTFORD TRAMWAY CO
- HIGHGATE HILL (CABLE) TRAMWAY LTD
- NORTH LONDON TRAMWAYS CO

- NORTH LONDON SUBURBAN TRAMWAYS CO
- HARROW ROAD & PADDINGTON TRAMWAYS CO LTD
- METROPOLITAN TRAMWAYS & OMNIBUS CO LTD
- SOUTHALL & SHEPHERDS BUSH TRAM RAILWAY CO LTD
- KEW RICHMOND & KINGSTON TRAMWAYS CO LTD
- THE LONDON & COUNTY TRAMWAYS CO LTD
- WEST METROPOLITAN TRAMWAYS CO

- LEA BRIDGE, LEYTON & WALTHAMSTOW TRAMWAYS CO

(4) The crest of the Metropolitan Railway Company, which incorporated the coats of arms of the City of London and the counties served by the line.

moved Morrison from office, the London Passenger Transport Bill was eventually passed and on 1st July 1933 the new authority came into being.

Under the new Board, powers of control were removed from the local authorities and the shareholders of the various companies involved. The shareholders received either cash payments or shares in the new undertaking, and their role in appointing the Chairman and Board was taken over by five 'appointing trustees', who included the Chairman of the LCC and the President of the Law Society. There was some public control over new developments, but real power rested with the Board. Its task, in the words of its first Chairman, Lord Ashfield, was *'to take such steps as it considers necessary for avoiding wasteful competitive services and for extending and improving London's passenger transport facilities so as to meet the growing needs of its vast population'*. 'London' as defined by the LPTB's operating area meant some 2,000 square miles within a 20–30 mile radius of Charing Cross and a population in 1933 rapidly approaching 9.5 million.

Some important decisions on future policy were taken almost immediately. At its first meeting on 6th July the Board decided to adopt diesel instead of petrol engines as standard for the bus fleet. It was estimated that this would save up to £120 a year per vehicle. As in so many other fields, London Transport set an important precedent here which was later followed by bus operators all over the country. For more than twenty years nearly all the General's buses had been built by the Associated Equipment Company (AEC), which was an off-shoot of the Underground group. Under the terms of the 1933 Act AEC became an independent company, but was contracted to supply 90 per cent of the LPTB's new chassis and spares over the next ten years. AEC was soon delivering an average of ten new buses a week, and by 1939 London Transport had replaced more than half the mixed fleet of older buses inherited in 1933–4 with new vehicles.

3

2

4

The Board also took an early decision to start replacing its trams with trolleybuses. In this it was persuaded by the successful operating experience of London United Tramways, which had been running a small trolleybus network in south-west London since 1931. Conversion to trolleybuses was cheaper than either modernising the system or replacing trams with diesel buses, as much of the electrical equipment could be re-used, but without the need for new track. Between 1935 and 1940 well over half London's huge tram network gave way to trolleybuses. Further conversion work had to be postponed because of the war, but in those five years the trolleybus system grew from just 18 route miles to 255 while the tramways were reduced to 102.

The most ambitious of London Transport's modernisation plans involved the Underground, where major improvements are always more expensive because of the huge capital costs of tunnelling and other large scale engineering works. A £40 million loan had to be raised, with government guarantees, to finance the 1935–40 New Works Programme. This was a joint scheme prepared by the LPTB and the main line railway companies consisting principally of extensions to the Bakerloo, Northern and Central Lines in north and east London. Some existing steam worked suburban branches of the London & North Eastern Railway were to be electrified and linked with the Underground to allow a through service of tube trains.

The achievements of the LPTB in its first six years were considerable. Hardly any part of the system remained untouched by the impressive programme of improvement and modernisation. The main exceptions were parts of the tramway network in south London, which were almost unchanged from the old LCC regime, and the outer sections of the Metropolitan Line. Beyond Rickmansworth, where all trains were still steam hauled, the atmosphere of a Victorian country railway survived in sharp contrast to the most up-to-date parts of the tube network. The quaint Brill branch, with its seventy-year-old locomotives, was closed in 1935 and the under-used service between Aylesbury and Verney Junction, more than fifty miles from central London, was withdrawn a year later. In 1937, the operation of all Met services beyond the limit of electric working was handed over to the LNER.

Two men in particular dominated London Transport in the thirties. The Chairman, Lord Ashfield, and his deputy Frank Pick between them already possessed more than half a century's management experience with the Underground group. Together, as Herbert Morrison commented, '*they made a formidable pair*'. Their combined administrative abilities, and Pick's special concern for the highest standards of design in every aspect of the Board's operations from stations and vehicles down to ticket machines and litter bins, helped to shape a transport system for London that was the envy of the world.

REFERENCE

Board's "Special Area."
Board's Area outside "Special Area."
Boundary of London Passenger Transport Area.
Boundary of London Traffic Area (1924).
Boundary of Metropolitan Police District.
Boundary of Administrative County of London.
Unrestricted Outward Runnings by the Board.
Restricted Outward Runnings by the Board.
Inward Runnings by Outside Proprietors.

(1) The Board's operating area covered nearly 2,000 square miles and stretched far beyond what most people consider to be London.

(2) Announcing the creation of London Transport, June 1933. The new authority inherited an Underground system on which nearly 416 million journeys were being made annually.

(3) Rush hour scene at Hammersmith in the early 1930s.

(1) The new undertaking explained its purpose in a series of press announcements. The winged LPTB symbol was apparently unpopular and was superseded within a year by the bullseye symbol already familiar to Underground travellers.

(2) Buses at the Bank, 1933. Nearly 6,000 buses passed into the ownership of the LPTB, many of which still had open staircases, a design hangover from horse bus days.

I

The London Passenger Transport Board has assumed control of most of the passenger transport undertakings which operate in an area within a radius of some 30 miles from Charing Cross. Its services include the underground railways, tramways, omnibuses and coaches.

1. The Purpose

The Board is a public authority appointed under Act of Parliament charged with responsibility for providing an adequate and properly co-ordinated system of passenger transport within the London Passenger Transport Area. It is required to take such steps as it considers necessary for avoiding wasteful, competitive services and for extending and improving London's passenger transport facilities, so as to meet the growing needs of the vast population working and dwelling within the area over which the Board's operations extend.

For all inquiries
LONDON PASSENGER
TRANSPORT BOARD
55, Broadway, Westminster,
S.W.1
Telephone: VICtoria 6800
Telegrams: Passengers Sowest London

2

This is No. 1 of a series of four announcements by the London Passenger Transport Board. Other announcements will be published at fortnightly intervals, as follows: 2. The Territory. 3. The Service. 4. The Staff.

17 JUL 1933

4

3

(3) Less than a month after the creation of London Transport, the last stage of the Piccadilly Line northern extension from Finsbury Park was opened. This was the short section from Enfield West (later renamed Oakwood) to Cockfosters.

(4) Charles Holden, who was largely responsible for the distinctive new architectural styles developed by the Underground from the mid-1920s, made effective use of reinforced concrete and glass in his design for the new Cockfosters station.

(1) Many of the 2,630 trams inherited by London Transport had been built before the First World War. This open-balconied London United Tramways car, seen at Shepherds Bush in 1933, dates from 1906, only five years after the LUT had opened London's first electric tram routes.

(2) The largest of the 17 tramway undertakings taken over by the LPTB was the London County Council's system, which covered 158 route miles. Typical of the LCC fleet was this 'E' class car built in 1906 and seen here at Mile End in 1934.

(3) The last major piece of tramway modernisation undertaken by the LCC had been the enlargement of the Kingsway subway in 1930-31 to take double-deck cars. The subway ran between the Embankment and Holborn (Southampton Row) with two intermediate underground 'stations' at Holborn and Aldwych.

(4) A glimpse of the future was given to suburban Londoners in 1931 when the London United Tramways opened a small network of trolleybus routes to replace trams in the Kingston area. The new vehicles proved cheaper to run than the trams and attracted more passengers. 61 LUT trolleybuses passed into London Transport's ownership in 1933.

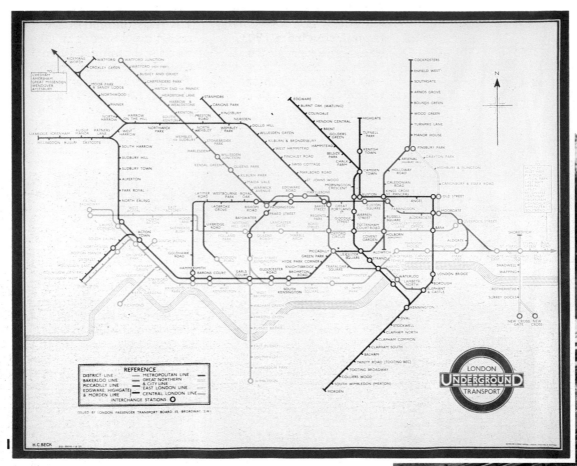

(*Main picture*) The Metropolitan was the only railway company taken over by London Transport that was not already part of the Underground group. Much of its rolling stock was still being built to traditional main line designs with wooden bodies, compartments and slam doors, such as this train of 1929 'MV' stock seen at Wembley Park en route for the newly opened Stanmore branch in 1933.

(**1**) The Underground system as it was at the end of 1933, the first year in which the map appeared in the diagrammatic form devised by Henry Beck. All subsequent versions of the diagram have been based on this ingenious design.

(2) The old and the new. A Central London Railway train dating from 1903 enters the new station at Holborn, opened in September 1933 to provide an interchange with the Piccadilly Line.

(3) The new and the old. The most modern tube trains on the system, known as 'standard' stock, were in service on the Piccadilly Line. Here passengers board a train of 1930 manufacture at the old District Railway South Harrow station, which was to be rebuilt in 1935.

(1 & 2) Under Frank Pick's enlightened direction London Transport carried on the Underground's tradition of explaining and promoting its activities through posters and exhibitions. For Pick this was more than a simple publicity exercise. As he saw it: *"The Board's undertaking is a declaration of faith that its task is worthwhile and that its labours shall eventually contribute their appointed share to the transformation of our urban civilisation into some fine flower of accomplishment."*

In 1933 there were fewer than 300,000 private cars licensed in the London Transport area, and most Londoners relied exclusively on public transport to travel to their work and leisure. The population of Greater London was still growing, but only in the suburban areas, where house building continued unabated by the Depression. Typical of London Transport services in the suburbs at this time are:

(3) A 1931-built 'Feltham' tramcar, the most modern type used in London, at Hillingdon.

(4) An 'A1' type trolleybus negotiating the new roundabout installed at Hampton Court when the trams were replaced.

(5) The bus/Underground interchange at Morden in 1936.

3

4

5

London Transport established a separate Country Bus and Coach division for its traffic area outside London. This included the Green Line express coach network created in 1930 by the General.

Two early London Transport Green Line posters of 1933 and 1935:

(1) *"Chess Valley"* by Henry Beck;

(2) *"It's Easy by Green Line"* by Laurence Bradshaw.

(3) One of the 'T' type Green Line coaches on the London to Baldock service (route AK) beside a new London Transport shelter in Stevenage High Street, August 1934.

(4) A Green Line coach stands with two 'ST' type double-deckers outside the Godstone garage of the East Surrey Traction Company shortly before take-over by London Transport in 1933.

Over the first five years of London Transport's operations the number of annual passenger journeys on the system increased by 10 per cent to almost 3,725 million.

(1) Arriving at Colindale by tube for an RAF Pageant at Hendon Aerodrome, June 1935.

(2) Crowding on to a tram on the Embankment, August 1934.

(3) Queueing for buses in the morning rush hour at London Bridge station, November 1933.

(4) Boarding a trolleybus at North Finchley, August 1939.

2

3

4

2

(1) A group of children board a special train at Ravenscourt Park to take them to the Pavilion Pleasure Grounds at Eastcote, July 1934.

(2) A 1935 poster by 'Herry' Perry.

3

4

(3) Adults too could enjoy a range of excursions organised by London Transport, such as this guided sightseeing coach tour.

(4) This poster advertising one of London's major tourist attractions was designed by Edward McKnight Kauffer in 1934.

E McKnight Kauffer

THE TOWER OF LONDON

The annual Derby Stakes at Epsom has always attracted large crowds.

(1) From the late 1920s onwards a special bus service to and from the racecourse was available on the day from Morden tube station. This tradition was continued by London Transport after 1933.

(2 & 3) A small fleet of old 'NS' type open-top buses was available for private party-hire, offering an excellent vantage point for the race and space for a comfortable picnic away from the crowds.

1

London Transport provided the cheapest and easiest means for most Londoners to get out into the country before the war.

2

LONDON TRANSPORT OPENS A WINDOW ON LONDON'S COUNTRY

(1) Epping Forest was a particularly popular choice for a leisurely Sunday or Bank Holiday excursion.

(2) Many of the 1930s posters, such as this example by Graham Sutherland, were designed to entice them out of the city.

(*Main picture*) The outer stations on the Metropolitan Line, such as Amersham, provided an ideal starting point for a ramble in the Chilterns. This section of 'Metroland' beyond Rickmansworth was still steam worked.

(3) It was even possible to make through bookings to Southend from Underground stations.

3

UNDERGROUND
METROPOLITAN LINE

CHEAP
FARES
TO
METRO-LAND
AND THE SEA

LONDON TRANSPORT

55, Broadway, S.W.I.
Victoria 6800.

March, 1934

(*Main picture*) The standard London bus of the thirties was the 'STL' type, originally designed by the General in 1932, but built for London Transport by AEC throughout the decade. By 1939 a total of 2,647 had been delivered, most of them with compression-ignition oil (diesel) engines which the LPTB had decided to adopt for nearly all of its new vehicles. The 'STLs' replaced older buses including the large 'NS' class, which had been the first covered-top double-deckers in London in the 1920s.

(1) A few 'NS' types were converted into service vehicles, such as this staff canteen in use at Victoria in 1937. Behind it are 'LT' and 'ST' type buses, the immediate predecessors of the 'STL'.

(2) The bus stop system was extended during the 1930s to cover the whole London Transport network. Until then it was still theoretically possible to hail a bus, like a taxi, almost anywhere.

(3 & 4) A bus driver and conductor display their new London Transport winter uniforms, January 1934.

One of the most advanced new bus designs in the 1930s was the 'Q' type which had made its debut with the LGOC in 1932. Its key innovative feature was the re-positioning of the engine behind the driver on the off-side of the chassis, which allowed more space for seating.

(1) The 'Q' was produced mainly as a single-decker for use in both the central and country areas, and as a Green Line coach.

(2) London Transport took delivery of only five double-deck versions, including Q3, one of the first buses to have a front entrance. This particular vehicle was destroyed by enemy action whilst in store at Swanley Garage in 1941.

In 1937 London Transport experimented with an underfloor-engined single-deck bus—the 'TF' type. Full production started in 1939 and most of the 88 vehicles built subsequently worked on the Green Line services operating from Romford and Grays Garages.

(3) TF77 has been preserved in running condition by the London Transport Museum.

1

2

(4) The LPTB bullseye device was ingeniously incorporated into the design of the radiator filler cap.

The most important bus to emerge from the LPTB drawing board in the 1930s was the 'RT'. This stylish new vehicle incorporated many advanced mechanical features including a pre-selective gearbox. Only 150 were delivered in 1939/40 before production was halted because of the war.

(5) The body of the prototype, RT1, has now been restored and mounted on a later chassis.

3

4

5

The LCC Tramways had always provided passenger shelters at many of its busy stops and interchange points, such as:

(1) New Cross Gate and **(2)** Stamford Hill.

London Transport carried on this tradition and extended it to bus and coach passengers. New shelters of a simplified design were introduced throughout the system from 1934.

(3) This example on the North Circular Road at Finchley shows the neat incorporation of map and timetable panels.

Many of the old bus garages inherited by London Transport were cramped and inadequate. The Board lost little time in rebuilding some which did not suit its operating requirements, particularly in the country area.

(4 & 5) Amersham Garage, which had been owned by the Amersham and District Bus Company, was rebuilt in 1935 with enlarged bus stabling and maintenance areas. The architects responsible for this and most of the other new garages were Wallis, Gilbert and Partners, better known at the time for their modern factory designs, which included the Firestone and Hoover plants in west London.

4

5

Within a few months of its establishment, London Transport announced plans to replace more trams with trolleybuses in the suburbs. After trials in 1934 with two experimental AEC trolleybuses, it was decided to standardise on large three-axle 70-seat vehicles for most of the new fleet. Orders were placed with both AEC and Leyland Motors, who between them were to supply all London's trolleybuses.

The first stage in the conversion programme was completed in late 1935, when two new trolleybus routes were inaugurated in west London.

(1) The last tram on former London United route 57 ran from Shepherd's Bush to Hounslow on the night of 26th October.

(2) The following morning trolleybuses on route 657 took over.

4

3

(3) Leyland Motors included this illustration of trolleybuses at Cricklewood in a 1936 brochure. Between 1935 and 1940 conversion of tram routes to trolleybus operation averaged 40 miles a year, until all but three had disappeared north of the Thames.

(4) In south-east London a small self-contained trolleybus network opened in November 1935 serving Dartford, Erith, Bexley and Woolwich (*shown here*).

1

2

3

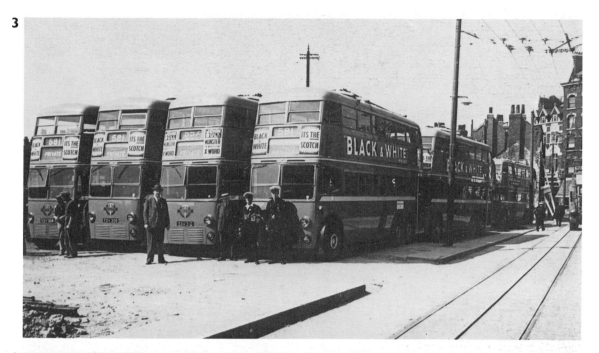

4

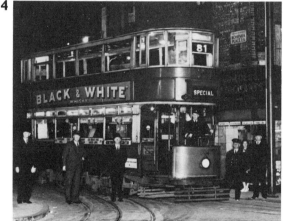

5

Although the electrical distribution system of the tramways could be utilised for trolleybuses, new twin overhead wiring was required. This was for the negative current return, which with trams was conducted through the running rails.

(1) New traction poles to support the overhead are seen here being installed at Ilford in 1938 using a specially built AEC Mercury pole carrier.

(2) The wiring was then fixed in position using tower wagons. Some of these vehicles, such as the pair in use here at Leyton in May 1939, were converted from old double-deck buses.

Tram routes were usually renumbered with a 5 or 6 prefix to the former route number when trolleybuses took over.

(3) At Hackney, for example, the newly delivered trolleybuses standing outside the depot in June 1939 carried route numbers 557 and 581 to replace ex-LCC tram routes 57 and 81.

(4) The last trams returned to Hackney depot on the night of 10th June.

(5) By this time much of the trackwork inside had already been removed.

(*Main picture*) At major road junctions where trolleybus routes crossed each other, a complicated overhead layout of 'frogs' (points) and cross-overs was inevitably required. In May 1937, five months after the last trams had negotiated this intersection between Blackhorse Road and Forest Road in Walthamstow, the disused track was still in position below the new trolleybus wires.

(1) A procession of trolleybuses at the Connaught Road terminus, West Ham, which served the then busy Royal Docks.

(2) By contrast, some trolleybuses ran right out into London's countryside, such as the 696 seen here in rural Kent en route for Dartford, the furthest point reached by trolleybuses south-east of the capital.

(3) For London Transport bus, tram and trolleybus crews summer officially began on 1st May when they had to start wearing white linen cap covers. The drivers were issued with white summer dustcoats.

(4) Trolleybus tickets in the 1930s followed the tradition of bus and tram tickets, with a different colour for each fare value and a complicated range of special journey issues.

(5) The trolleybus symbol was applied to every vehicle in the fleet.

1

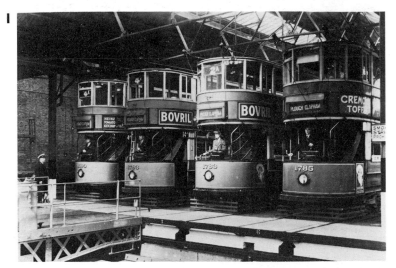

2

3

4

(1) It was still necessary to train new tram drivers in the 1930s, a task seen here being carried out at the former LCC Clapham Depot.

(2) Many of them later had to be re-trained for the more complex manoeuvres involved in trolleybus driving. A scene at Fulwell Depot in November 1935.

(3) Bus drivers continued to be instructed on the famous Chiswick skid patch, often using obsolete vehicles.

(4) Their conductors had to be trained in the complicated procedure of fare collection and ticket issue using Bell Punch machines.

(5) Staff had to maintain a smart appearance at all times!

(6) Once their training was completed crews were allocated to a particular bus garage or tram/trolleybus depot. Conductors are seen here making up their waybills (records of takings) and paying in the money at the end of their period of duty at Upton Park Garage in August 1933.

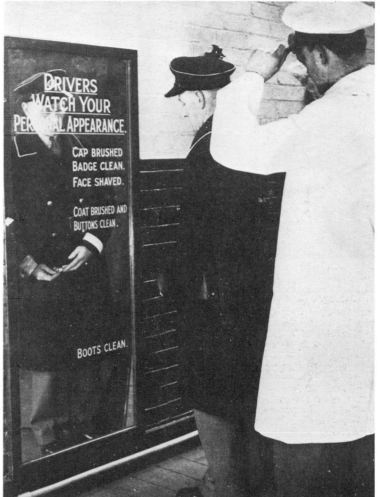

5

6

(1) The old staff magazine of the Underground Group was replaced by a monthly London Transport publication from January 1934. Its new title was 'Pennyfare', then the general rate per mile on London's buses and trams. After the war it was renamed 'London Transport Magazine'.

(2) In June 1939 'Pennyfare' reported the first ride on the Underground by the young princesses. For Princess Elizabeth, the experience was not to be repeated until, as Queen Elizabeth II, she opened the Victoria Line 30 years later.

(3) An earlier Royal occasion, the Coronation of her father King George VI in May 1937, had been a less happy experience for London Transport. Elaborate preparations had been made to run special bus services on Coronation Day, and a commemorative poster by Harold Stabler issued. However, central area bus crews, who had been on strike for better working conditions since

2

PENNYFARE

Vol. VI. No. 6   STAFF JOURNAL OF LONDON TRANSPORT   June 1939

Princesses Go
UNDERGROUND
2d. THIRD-CLASS TICKETS

Re-entering Tottenham Court Road Station and (left) In St. James Park Station

As the newspaper heading at the top shows, on May 15 Princess Elizabeth and Princess Margaret Rose made a journey by Underground, their first. They travelled with a Lady-in-Waiting and their Governess from St. James Park to Tottenham Court Road and back. Both Princesses were greatly interested in the escalators, automatic ticket-machines and automatic doors. It is understood that the journey was part of a new plan for their education.

CORONATION DAY 12 MAY

1st May, continued their industrial action throughout the month. No red buses ran on 12th May, and crews only returned to work on the 28th when the dispute was settled by a Court of Inquiry.

(4) This photograph shows busmen at Victoria back at work after the strike.

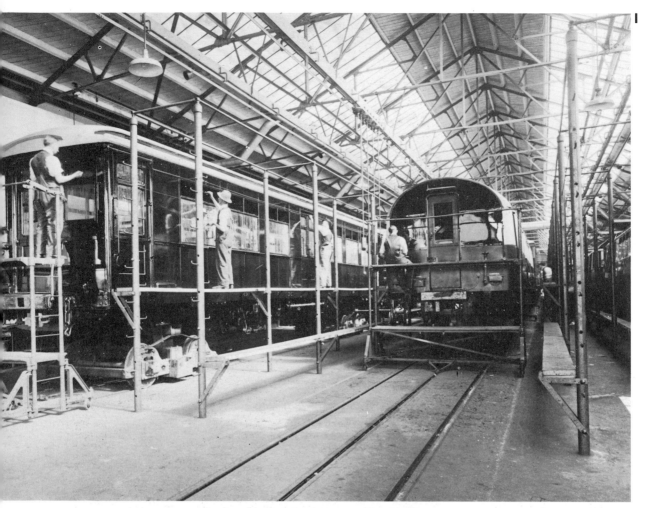

(1) The main servicing and repair works for the Underground in the 1930s was (and still is) at Acton, where rolling stock was fully overhauled, on average, every two years. Car bodies were removed from their bogies and both elements were then repaired where necessary, repainted and reassembled on constantly moving 'production lines'.

(2) The bus division's equivalent to Acton, on an adjacent site, was Chiswick Works, where in addition to bus overhaul facilities, back up services such as the destination blind shop were located.

Day-to-day maintenance of all road and rail vehicles was carried out in their home garages and depots. Facilities for such work were considerably improved in the 1930s, especially where new premises had been constructed, as shown here.

(3) Cockfosters Rolling Stock Depot built for the Piccadilly Line extension in 1933.

(4) Bexleyheath Trolleybus Depot completed in 1935.

(5) Addlestone Country Bus Garage opened in 1936.

1

4

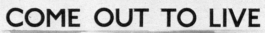

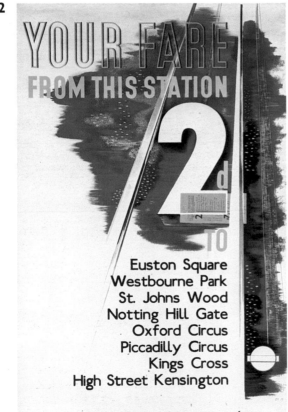

2

3

Season ticket sales increased by almost 15 per cent in the Board's first five years, reaching a peak of nearly 77.3 million in 1938.

(1) Regular Underground travel, and the purchase of season tickets in particular, was promoted by a series of striking posters by leading modern artists including:

(2) Laszlo Moholy-Nagy

(3) Paul Nash

(4) Zero (Hans Schleger).

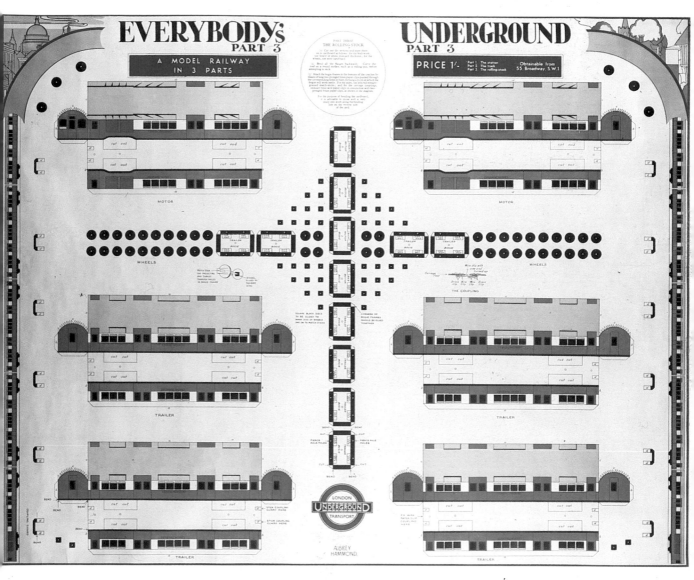

(5) Even children were included in the publicity campaign with this cut-out card model of a tube train.

3

The growing number of passengers using the Underground in the early 1930s led to some overcrowding especially on the Morden–Edgware (Northern) Line, and this, together with plans for extending the network, necessitated a radical re-appraisal of tube train design.

(1) The most important change, which was incorporated in four experimental trains ordered from Metro-Cammell in 1935, was the relocation of the motor driving equipment, previously housed behind

2

the driver's cab. This was now positioned under the floor creating valuable additional space for passenger seating.

(2) The first three new trains delivered in 1936 were built with fully streamlined cab ends.

1

4

(3) The fourth had a more conventional appearance. Operating trials showed that the streamlining had little advantage at the relatively low speeds reached by tube trains and it was the flat-fronted design which was adopted as standard.

(4) A huge fleet of tube trains, eventually totalling over 1,200 cars, was built from 1938 onwards to replace the existing trains on the Bakerloo and Northern Lines. One of the first units to be delivered is seen here on a test run at Acton Town in 1938.

5

(5) New trains with smoother, less cluttered, body styling than previous stock were also designed for the 'surface' Underground lines (Metropolitan, District and Circle) and delivery of these commenced in 1937.

1

CHANCERY LANE NEW STATION

OPEN JUNE 25

OPEN JUNE 25

NEW ENTRANCES
NEW TICKET HALL
NEW ESCALATORS

LONDON TRANSPORT

Station rebuilding, started by the Underground in the mid-1920s, continued after 1933. Some of the busiest stations in central London were completely reconstructed with new escalators and sub-surface ticket halls.

(1) Chancery Lane on the Central Line was reopened in June 1934.

(2) Leicester Square, where the new booking hall followed the circular pattern first used at Piccadilly Circus in 1928, was completed in 1935.

(3) The escalator to the Piccadilly Line at Leicester Square was at that time claimed to be the longest and fastest in the world.

2

3

4

In the western suburbs two stations on the Piccadilly Line were rebuilt in new locations to allow direct access from recently opened arterial roads.

(4) Park Royal on the Western Avenue was completed in 1936.

(5 & 6) At Osterley, the old District Railway station of 1883 was closed in 1934 when a new station designed by Charles Holden was opened nearby on the Great West Road. A car park accommodating over 50 vehicles was provided to encourage motorists to complete their journeys to central London by tube.

5

6

The distinctive 'house-style' created by Charles Holden was applied to all the new stations built in the 1930s. Frank Pick insisted on careful attention to the design of every detail so that all features were both functional and an integral part of the overall scheme.

(1) Clear illuminated signs, bronze tubular handrails and 'biscuit' coloured tiling were the stylish hallmarks of the rebuilt stations, such as Earls Court, which was partially reconstructed in 1937 with a new entrance to serve the new exhibition hall.

(2) When Eastcote station was rebuilt in 1936 the new design incorporated a row of shops at street level in the same architectural style.

(3) At Boston Manor in 1934 an illuminated tower was provided to identify the station at night.

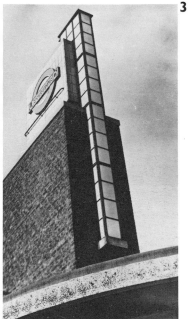

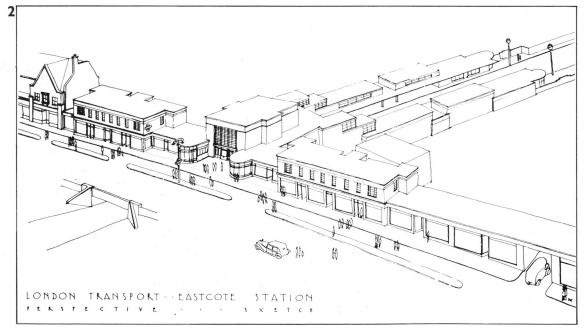

LONDON TRANSPORT · EASTCOTE STATION
PERSPECTIVE . . . SKETCH

(4 & 5) The first part of the 1935–40 New Works Programme to be completed was the Bakerloo Line extension from Baker Street to Finchley Road, where it joined the Metropolitan Line tracks and ran via Wembley Park to Stanmore. All the new and rebuilt stations on the line were designed by London Transport's staff architect Stanley Heaps, but in the established Holden mould.

(6) The Bakerloo service to Stanmore began on 20th November 1939, using the newly constructed dive-under below the Met main line at Wembley Park.

4

5

6

(1) The Piccadilly Line had been extended over Metropolitan Line tracks to Uxbridge in October 1933 and it soon became apparent that the old Belmont Road terminus was too small to cope with the additional traffic.

(2) A large new station with three platforms, similar in design to Cockfosters, was built closer to the town centre in the High Street and opened in December 1938.

1

2

3

4

(3) A particularly striking feature of Holden's design was a heraldic stained glass window in the booking hall by Erwin Bossanyi, incorporating the coats' of arms of Uxbridge Urban District Council and the counties of Middlesex and Buckinghamshire.

(4 & 5) The old Post Office station was rebuilt in 1939 and renamed St. Paul's. The style followed that of Chancery Lane, but with the addition of some decorative tiles with moulded relief devices designed by Harold Stabler. These depicted the cathedral, the LPTB Head Office at 55 Broadway and other London landmarks, as well as coats of arms and the LPTB bullseye and griffin symbols.

5

A major part of the 1935–40 New Works Programme was the extension of the Northern Line to link up with and take over the London & North Eastern Railway's steam worked branches to High Barnet, Edgware and Alexandra Palace.

(1) By 1938 tunnelling had been completed from Highgate (Archway) to the surface at East Finchley, making the 17-mile tunnel from there to Morden, via Bank, the longest in the world at that time.

(2) The old LNER station at East Finchley was rebuilt, but had not been completed when the tube service was inaugurated in July 1939.

(3 & 4) Holden's new station was finished in 1940 and incorporated an archer figure by Eric Aumonier as a decorative feature. In April 1941, by which time tube trains were running through to High Barnet and Mill Hill East, the new split-level interchange station at Highgate was opened. All further work on the extension then had to be suspended due to the war.

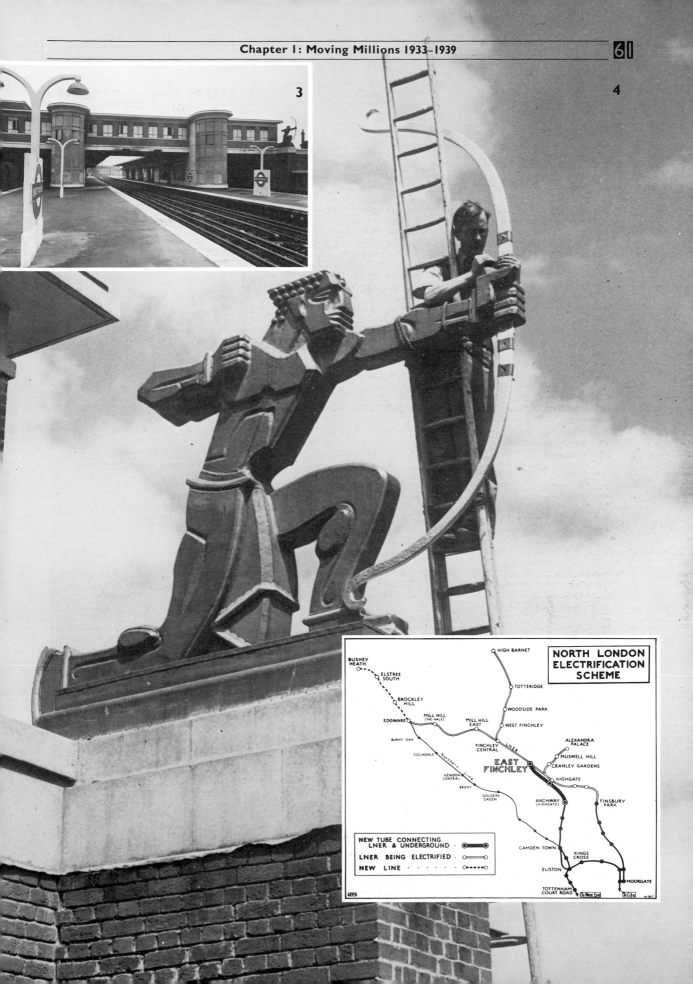

In the 1930s, with television in its infancy, more Londoners took advantage of bus and Underground services to have an evening out in town, encouraged no doubt by posters such as these striking examples designed by:

(1) A. Severin, 1938

(2) Tom Eckersley and Eric Lombers, 1935.

CHAPTER
2
The War Years
1939-1945

THE PROUD CITY

A NEW VIEW OF ST. PAUL'S CATHEDRAL FROM BREAD STREET

"...the principal Ornament of our royal City,
to the Honour of our Government, and
of this our Realm...."

Letters Patent under the Great Seal of England the 12th day Nov. 1673.

(*Previous page*) A wartime poster by Walter Spradbery, 1944.

At 11.15am on 3rd September 1939, households all over Britain tuned in their wireless sets for a broadcast from the Prime Minister, Neville Chamberlain. He began with these now famous words: '*I am speaking to you from the Cabinet Room at No. 10 Downing Street. This morning, the British Ambassador in Berlin handed the German government a final note, stating that unless the British government heard from them by 11 o'clock that they were prepared at once to withdraw their troops from Poland, a state of war would exist between us. I have to tell you now that no such undertaking has been received, and that consequently this country is at war with Germany.*'

The announcement came as no surprise. War with Nazi Germany as a result of Hitler's aggression towards neighbouring countries had seemed increasingly likely for months. Exactly a year earlier, during the Munich Crisis, hostilities had been averted at the last moment by Chamberlain's 'piece of paper' agreement with Hitler, but it soon became clear that this had only postponed the inevitable conflict. The borrowed time did at least allow some preparations to be taken against the expected aerial bombardment by the Luftwaffe. London Transport, like most large organisations, had followed government instructions and appointed an Air Raid Precautions Committee as early as 1937. By September 1938, when the Munich Crisis arose, the Board had drawn up detailed defence plans which would allow the system to remain operational under aerial attack, with the safety of passengers and staff secured as far as possible. A year later ARP arrangements came into effect on Friday 1st September, two days before the official declaration of war.

The first major task for London Transport was to assist in the mass evacuation of London's children, hospital patients and expectant mothers to the safety of the country. Nearly 13,000 evacuees were ferried to Waterloo alone by bus, tram and tube for transfer on to main line trains. In other cases the Board's buses and coaches were used for the whole journey and many drivers had no sleep for 36 hours. A national Railway Executive Committee came into being to oversee the operation of both the LPTB and the main line railways, though the existing management continued. Blackout restrictions were applied immediately, and London Transport's petrol and oil supplies were cut by 25 per cent as an economy measure. Bus services were heavily restricted or withdrawn altogether to save fuel and limit blackout working, and within four months more than 800 central area buses were lying idle. Some Green Line coach services, all of which had been withdrawn on 1st September, were being restored by this time, although they were to be cut out again in 1942. Underground, trolleybus and tram services also had to be reduced, but fortunately there was a considerable reduction in passenger demand because of the effect of the war on business and the evacuation of many offices.

(1) Early precautions against bomb blasts taken before hostilities began included filling in certain subway entrances with ballast.

(2) Flood gates were installed in the tunnels under the Thames at Charing Cross (Embankment) and Waterloo stations.

More than half the modernisation and improvement work scheduled under the 1935–40 programme had been carried out by the autumn of 1939. Some of it continued during the first year of the war, though at a reduced level. The last tram to trolleybus conversion, in the Poplar area, was completed in June 1940 and some work on the Northern Line extension went on until the following year, but most new tasks undertaken by London Transport's engineers from 1939 onwards were directly concerned with the war. Tube stations in the central area, and the tunnels under the Thames, were protected against flooding in the event of the river, sewers or water mains being breached after bombing by the installation of floodgates and watertight doors. Disused platforms and passageways at a number of central Piccadilly Line stations were converted into emergency headquarters offices for the Board and the Railway Executive Committee, one of which was later used for meetings of the War Cabinet during the Blitz. Operations rooms for London's Anti-Aircraft Command were also established deep in a tube station within a few feet of the passing trains.

London Transport staff had been receiving regular ARP training in rescue, fire fighting and first aid since before the war, but in May 1940 the Board also formed its own Home Guard unit, which eventually had nearly 30,000 members. As growing numbers of male staff were called up for service in the Forces, the Board began to recruit more female staff to replace them. Women enthusiastically took on virtually every job previously reserved for men, including labouring and heavy engineering work, though they were not allowed to become drivers.

The long expected air raids finally began in the summer of 1940. The first bombs to damage London Transport equipment hit New Malden on 16th August, and immediately demonstrated the vulnerability of the trolleybus system to aerial attack by bringing down a section of the overhead. Heavy bombing started on 7th September with a daylight raid on the Docks and East End. London was then bombed every night until 2nd November, after which the Blitz continued intermittently until May 1941. In 57 raids the Luftwaffe dropped some 13,500 tons of high explosive and incendiary bombs, killing more than 15,000 civilians. For every person killed, another 35 were made homeless.

The damage and disruption to the London Transport system was severe, but never crippling. A service of some kind could nearly always be maintained, though this was more difficult with the trams and the Underground when trackwork and tunnels were hit. Buses could always be diverted, and this was even possible with trolleybuses. Wherever necessary, maintenance crews erected new traction poles and overhead quickly and efficiently, often working on their tower wagons while the Blitz raged around them. The average time taken to reinstate the trolleybus service after an 'incident' was only four hours.

(1) The Air Raid Precautions Manual issued to all London Transport staff from 1938 onwards.

(2) The appearance of the familiar London bus underwent several changes after war broke out. The 'LT' type shown in this reconstructed Second World War setting is now on permanent display in wartime condition at the London Transport Museum, Covent Garden.

As soon as the Blitz started, thousands of Londoners took to the tubes for shelter. At first this was not officially encouraged, and as no special facilities had been installed or arrangements made, there were chaotic scenes. Mass Observation, the social study organisation, reported that *'for the first time in many hundreds of years civilised families conducted the whole of their leisure and domestic lives in full view of each other. . . . Most of these people were not merely sheltering in the tubes; they were living there'*. In the newly completed Central Line extension tunnels east of Liverpool Street, where trains were not yet running, there was no compulsion for shelterers to leave during the day, and many stayed down for weeks on end. Gradually sheltering facilities became properly organised with special admission tickets, bunk beds, refreshments and, at some stations, libraries, music and live entertainment. At one there was even a newspaper, *The Swiss Cottager*, produced by the local shelterers' committee. The Underground tunnels were not entirely safe from attack, however, and shelterers were killed in six separate bomb incidents when tube stations were hit. On Government instructions, London Transport began building eight new tunnels at a deeper level in 1940. These were to act as more secure public shelters while the war continued, but there were long-term plans to use them as the basis for new express tube lines. In fact, the tunnels were used exclusively for military purposes from their completion in 1942 until the flying bomb attacks in 1944 when five were opened up as civilian shelters. The express tube idea was never implemented.

London Transport not only transported and sheltered both civilians and military personnel; it also made an important contribution to the war effort through its workshops. The London Aircraft Production group was set up in 1941 in association with four motor companies—Chrysler, Duple, Express Motor and Body Works and Park Royal Coach Works—to build Halifax heavy bombers. More than 700 were manufactured over a four year period by a workforce of whom 80 per cent had no previous engineering experience. Over half of them were women. London Transport's building department made parts for trestle bridges, landing craft, pontoon floats and aircraft turntables. The engineering shops at Charlton tram and trolleybus overhaul works were turned over to the manufacture of ammunition and gun parts, while the bus and coach department built nearly a thousand lorries, overhauled War Department vehicles and made parts for tanks. At Acton railway works, London Transport overhauled landing craft motors and carried out repair work on tanks, converting many for operation in water up to ten feet deep. This work reached a peak in the months leading up to the Allied invasion of Europe in June 1944. As 'D' Day approached, London Transport buses conveyed six infantry divisions to their ships and assault craft at the Channel ports. Over the next few weeks many of them were required again to transfer returning army casualties from trains to hospitals.

2

3

4

(3) Over 400 Green Line coaches were converted into ambulances within four hours of the suspension of coach services in September 1939.

(4) In October 1938 the LPTB had formed its own Territorial Army unit, the 84th (London Transport) Heavy Anti-Aircraft Regiment. Two batteries are seen here on parade at Stonebridge Park

Trolleybus Depot prior to attending their first camp in August 1939, only a month before war was declared.

(1 & 2) Plans for the mass evacuation of children, hospital patients and expectant mothers from London had been drawn up well in advance of hostilities. Evacuation began on 1st September 1939 and within four days 607,000 people had been carried out of the capital or to main line railway stations by London Transport buses, Underground trains and trams.

(3) The Green Line coach ambulances, which could each carry up to ten stretcher cases, moved patients out of the sandbagged central London hospitals either direct to King Edward VII Hospital at Windsor or to convenient railheads for transfer on to the Southern Railway.

GOOD BYE TRANSPORT

With no air raids during the early months of the war about a third of the evacuees soon returned to London.

(4) Another exodus took place in the summer of 1940, however, after the German invasion of Holland and Belgium, when enemy air raids on London seemed inevitable, and again during the flying bomb attacks in 1944. When London was safe again the evacuees came home.

By this time London was under attack from a sinister new weapon, the 'V1' flying bomb. The heaviest 'V1' assaults were between June and August 1944, but from 8th September the Germans began using the more powerful 'V2' rocket bombs as well and continued to hit London until the end of March 1945. Damage was much less serious than during the Blitz of 1940–41, but the final months of bombing prompted another wave of evacuation and contributed to a new reduction in London Transport's passenger carrying levels, which had increased again in 1942–43 with greater mobilisation for war work and the arrival of US Forces in London. Quite apart from the enormous problems involved in trying to maintain services with badly damaged vehicles and property, London Transport was finding itself unable to cover its costs in 1944–45. By the end of the war fares had gone up by 10 per cent, but costs had soared by 45 per cent. When 'VE' (Victory in Europe) Day dawned on 8th May 1945 London Transport could proudly claim to have 'carried on' throughout the worst periods of the six year war, but it was clear that new challenges lay ahead.

2

3

4

Blackout regulations were imposed from 1st September 1939, giving London a ghostly, eerie look after dark.

(1) Buses, like all other road vehicles, had to be fitted with headlamp cowls which reduced the beam to narrow slits. With street lighting also restricted, driving at night became quite hazardous.

(2 & 3) Two London Transport blackout posters of 1942.

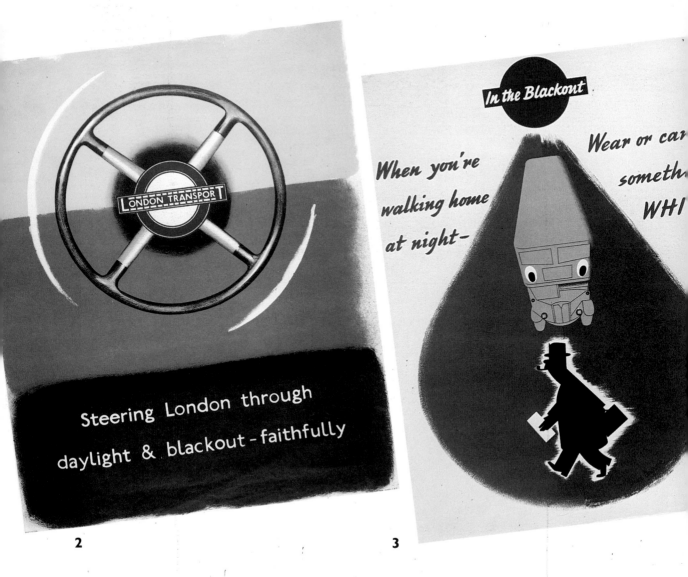

2

3

(4 & 5) Netting was glued to the windows of all London Transport vehicles to reduce splintering from bomb blasts. Interior lighting was reduced as a further blackout precaution, making it difficult for passengers to read and for conductors to check that they were being offered the correct fare.

(6) It was thought likely that the Germans would use gas in their attacks on London, but fortunately this threat never materialised.

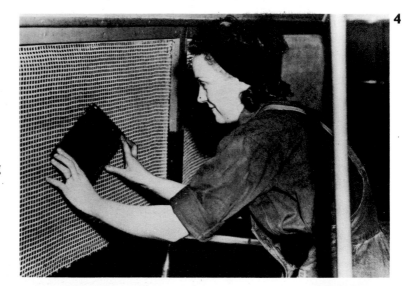

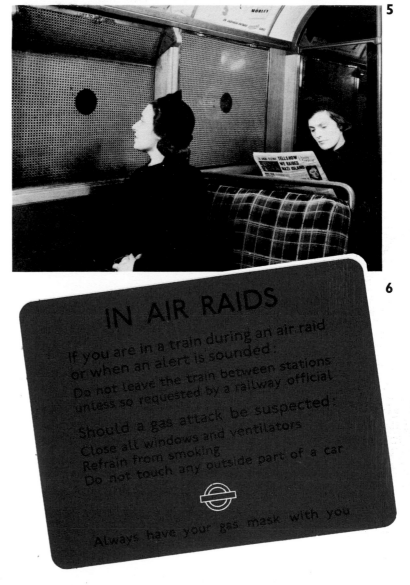

IN AIR RAIDS

If you are in a train during an air raid or when an alert is sounded:
Do not leave the train between stations unless so requested by a railway official

Should a gas attack be suspected:
Close all windows and ventilators
Refrain from smoking
Do not touch any outside part of a car

Always have your gas mask with you

During the six years of war more than 22,000 male staff were called up for service in the armed forces, and to replace them London Transport recruited men over the call-up age and 16,500 additional female staff. The women were employed in a variety of tasks, including many which had been exclusively male preserves before the the war.

Their work included: (*background picture*) bus chassis assembly,

(1) vehicle cleaning,

(2) motor-cycle despatch riding,

(3) station platform duties,

(4) signal box assistance,

(5) and, of course, bus conducting, a job which many women had undertaken in the First World War.

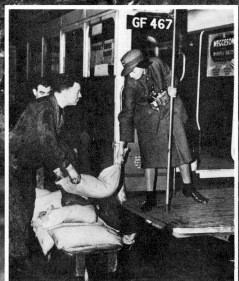

1

2

SHELTER
IN UNDERGROUND STATIONS

ADMISSION OF SHELTERERS

Shelterers will not be admitted to this station until 6.30 p.m.

At 6.15 a.m. shelterers must withdraw to the line 4ft. from the wall, and leave the station entirely by 7 a.m. weekdays and 8 a.m. Sundays

SHELTER TICKETS

All shelterers must have either

1. A PERIOD RESERVATION TICKET

Issued free by the local authority in whose area the station is situated. Entitles the holder to reserved accommodation for shelter each night; or

2. A CASUAL SHELTER TICKET

Issued free at the ticket office, subject to accommodation being available. Admits the holder to the station at which it is issued for shelter for one night only. Must be given up when the holder leaves the station

Neither of these tickets is available for travel by train. Both are issued subject to the conditions printed on them.

3

LONDON TRANSPORT in conjunction
with The LOCAL AUTHORITY
Admit one Person for Shelter
(if available) at
WOOD GREEN Station
Persons permitted to use this
Station as, or as a means of access to, an
Air Raid Shelter do so at their own risk
in all respects.
FOR FURTHER CONDITIONS SEE BACK

TL 1985

The first sporadic air raids on London by the Luftwaffe were carried out in August 1940 and from September onwards heavy 'blitz' bombing took place regularly until the summer of 1941.

(1) Although officially it was intended not to allow people to shelter in tube stations, in practice it was difficult to stop them. By the end of September it was estimated that more than 175,000 people were taking cover in deep level tube stations every night, sleeping wherever they could when trains and escalators stopped running.

(2 & 3) The initial chaos gradually disappeared as ordered arrangements for sheltering were made between London Transport and the local authorities.

4

5

6

(4) By early 1941 bunk-beds sleeping over 20,000 people had been installed at 79 stations.

(5) Refreshments were provided at many of the stations, delivered during the day by special trains.

(6) First aid and medical posts were also set up by the local authorities in whose areas the stations were situated.

(7) Strict rules covered every aspect of the sheltering activity!

7

SHELTERERS' BEDDING
The practice of shaking bedding over the platforms, tracks and in the subways is strictly forbidden

I

Billy's Bulletin

in the black-out tonight wear something WHITE

No. ABB 1234   THIS YEAR, NEXT YEAR   A CRUSADE FOR WISER TRAVEL   PRICELESS

All the Browns (and Brownes) Agree—

LOOK OUT IN THE BLACK-OUT IS THE BEST POLICY

WHEN Billy Brown goes out at night he wears or carries something white. When Mrs. Brown is in the black-out she likes to wear her old white mack out.

And Sally Brown straps round her shoulder a natty plain white knick-knack holder.

. . . so they may be seen at night

The reason why they wear this white is so they may be seen at night.

Down below the station's bright, but here outside it's black as night. Billy Brown will wait a bit and let his eyes grow used to it. Then he'll scan the road and see,

before he crosses, if it's free; remembering when lights are dim that cars he sees may not see him.

The safest travelling in town is not too good for Billy Brown. He's much too sensible and knowing to jump down off a bus that's going, especially in black-out hours, or when the kerb is wet with showers. On these occasions Billy B. goes by the slogan 'Wait and See.'

Cars he sees may not see him

WHAT'S IN A NAME?

THE answer is Everything—if you use it to good purpose, as Billy Brown does.

QUIZ CORNER Says Billy Brown, 'It seems to me that things get lost quite needlessly. Because they bear no name inside they cannot be identified. *My name and address are found on everything I take around,* and so I'm very pleased to see you think it wise to copy me.'

Billy Brown has had a rise in bus men's estimation Since he paid the fare exact and named his destination

Billy Brown's Own Highway Code—

He flags his bus with something white

for black-outs is 'Stay off the Road'. He'll never step out and begin to meet a bus that's pulling in. He doesn't wave his torch at night, but 'flags' his bus with something white. He never jostles in a queue, but waits and takes his turn—
Do you?

His slogan : *Wait and See.*

PATTERN SHOPPER

'YOU see, my dear', said Billy Brown, 'how transport services in town begin their main rush-hours by 4 (much earlier than before the war). And so, when shopping it's my view that you, and other shoppers too, should try to start for home by 3.' 'I will, my dear', said Mrs. B.

For copper rides, says Billy Brown, I never tender half-a-crown : The right amount saves much delay And speeds the tram upon its way

That's the Stuff (*It may Save YOUR LIFE*)

IN the train a fellow sits and pulls the window-net to bits, because the view is somewhat dim, a fact which seems to worry him.

As Billy cannot bear the sight, he says 'My man, that is not right. **I trust you'll pardon my correction:** That stuff is there for your protection.'

No Jam

NOT for our hero, anyhow. Not the sort of jam that spills out of a bottle-neck of overflowing traffic. But read on.

Billy finds it quite a strain to get himself inside a train: with such a squash around the door there's hardly room for any more. But down the car there's heaps of space and everyone could find a place. 'So let's all move along', says Billy: '*to crowd the entrance up is silly.*'

Many or few, it's BETTER TO QUEUE

BILLY'S standing in a queue, as we all must sometimes do. Queueing in these days of rush means **you don't have any crush,** and the seconds saved will lend extra wings to journey's end. But, says Billy, see you choose the proper one of several queues!

---Today's---
GOOD
---Deed---

WHEN you travel to and fro, on a line you really know, remember those who aren't so sure and haven't been that way before. Do your good deed for the day — *tell them the stations on the way.*

THE WORLD'S MOST EXEMPLARY PASSENGER

When travelling on the Underground, you must have noticed, I'll be bound, little notes of friendly warning which one looks at every morning, referring to a Billy Brown, a citizen of London Town—a bloke who always does things right, a chap whose torch is not too bright, who scans his black-out every night, won't drive a car if he gets tight . . .

Now Billy, I have heard it said, would shake a disapproving head at those who never can refrain from scratching at the window pane. A glance would say, in their direction, 'This is here for your protection.' Of netted glass we see about the same is true, without a doubt. A time may come amidst the strife, when covered windows save a life . . .

Let us, then, not be forgetting of this, our duty to the netting.

Printed by Waterlow & Sons Limited, London, E.C.2, and published by London Transport at the Sign of the ⊕ 55 Broadway, London, S.W.1.

Face the driver ▬ ▬ ▬
Face the driver ▬ ▬ ▬

Do you use the B B Sign?

Hail your bus or tram in the correct way.

Face the driver, raise you hand— You'll find that he will understand

STOP PRESS
'No Smoking' Rule Breach Significant Incident

At Bow Street Police Court to-day Billy Brown was commended by magistrate for frustrating attempt by passenger on Underground to smoke in car labelled 'No Smoking.'

LONDON TRANSPORT

Travel in wartime was quite different from anything people had experienced before.

(I) In an attempt to give passengers useful advice and relieve some of the gloom of blackout journeys on restricted services, London Transport issued a series of posters featuring 'Billy Brown of London Town', a pompous little cartoon character created by David Langdon. Not surprisingly, these rhyming couplets concerning 'The World's Most Exemplary Passenger' prompted the appearance of some rather wittier replies in the form of graffiti.

2

(2) Queueing for buses outside Sidcup Garage, October 1943.

3

(3) The interior of a wartime trolleybus. This particular vehicle was the first of 42 built for export to Durban and Johannesburg, but diverted for service in London because of the war, and in the event never delivered to South Africa.

4

(4) Despite the hostilities, London Transport continued to carry out design experiments on rolling stock. This District Line car was the first to be fitted with fluorescent lighting in October 1944.

3

(1) Throughout the war priority was given to essential travel. Posters were produced by the Railway Executive Committee designed to dissuade civilians from making unnecessary journeys.

(2) This poster by Fougasse stressed the inconvenience that delays could cause to other passengers.

(3 & *main picture***)** Members of the British and Allied Armed Forces were issued with special day tickets for use when on leave in uniform.

(3) A bomb which penetrated the station concourse at the Bank on 11th January 1941 killed 56 people and injured 69. A huge crater was left, over which a temporary Bailey Bridge had to be built for road traffic.

(*Main picture*) By far the worst incident occurred at Balham on the evening of 14th October 1940, when a bomb exploded below ground in the tube station. Mains were fractured, flooding the station with water, gravel and escaping gas. 64 shelterers and four

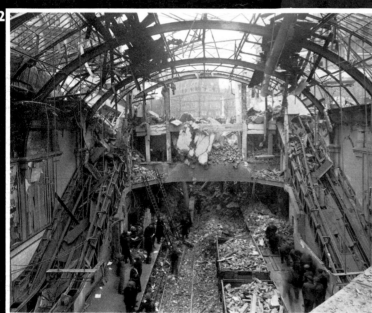

Nearly 50,000 high explosive bombs and millions of incendiaries fell on London during the blitz of 1940/41.

(1 & 2) Sloane Square station, which had been newly equipped with escalators in March 1940, was almost completely destroyed during an air raid on 12th November.

railwaymen were found dead in the debris and it was three months before the line could be re-opened.

(4 & 5) On the surface tram tracks in Balham High Road were badly damaged and the force of the explosion blew a bus into the bomb crater.

Bomb damage was often dramatic and caused severe disruption to many services.

These views show the devastation after air raids in September 1940 at:

(1) Islington.

(2) Clapham tram depot.

(3) Plaistow station.

(4) In many cases it was possible to repair and rebuild even quite badly damaged vehicles.

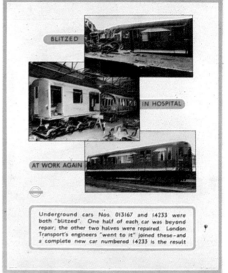

BLITZED

IN HOSPITAL

AT WORK AGAIN

Underground cars Nos. 013167 and 14233 were both "blitzed". One half of each car was beyond repair; the other two halves were repaired. London Transport's engineers "went to it" joined these – and a complete new car numbered 14233 is the result

5

6

The ARP training which London Transport staff had received proved vital during the Blitz of 1940–41.

(5) Fire fighting was an important aspect of the training, much of which was undertaken by staff in their spare time.

(6) As far as possible regular services were maintained throughout the bomb-damaged capital, but diversions were often inevitable after heavy raids.

(7) A series of London Transport posters by Walter Spradbery issued in 1944 celebrated the city's survival.

7

THE PROUD CITY

CHELSEA POWER HOUSE FROM MEEK STREET

"...the poor buildings lose themselves in the dim sky, and the tall chimneys become campanili, and the warehouses are palaces in the night, and the whole city hangs in the heavens..."
James McNeill Whistler

(1 & 2) Vehicle shortages as a result of the bombing led to an urgent appeal by London Transport in October 1940 for assistance from provincial bus operators. Within a week 472 buses had arrived on loan from other parts of the country. The last of them went back in June 1941, but as German bombing was subsequently directed against new targets in the provinces, London Transport was later able to offer 334 of its own buses to other cities.

(3) In an attempt to conserve fuel, 160 buses were converted to run on producer gas generated by burning anthracite in trailer units towed behind the vehicles. Although this system was successful in saving more than three million gallons of fuel, improvements in the availability of fuel supplies, coupled with difficulties experienced in operating the producer gas system, led to its abandonment in the autumn of 1944.

1

2

3

(4 & 5) Commercial vehicle production ceased shortly after the outbreak of war, but from 1942 the Ministry of Supply authorised the construction of a limited number of new buses. Guy Motors Ltd built most of the chassis and several coach building firms supplied the somewhat austere bodies, many of which were fitted with wooden-slatted seats.

4

5

(6) A short-lived emergency river-boat service between Westminster and Woolwich was provided by London Transport in the autumn of 1940 because of severe disruption to tram and trolleybus power supplies caused by bombing.

6

Throughout the war new staff had to be recruited to replace those in the Forces.

(2) The morale of those who kept the services going was sustained by posters such as this example by Fred Taylor.

(*Main picture* & **1**) London Transport staff raised enough money to pay for two Spitfires, both of which carried the LPTB 'bullseye' symbol.

LONDON TRANSPORT

SPITFIRE FUND

SUBSCRIPTION FORMS ARE NOW OBTAINABLE FROM THE PAYMASTER

GET YOURS, GIVE WHAT YOU CAN AND KEEP GIVING

One Spitfire = £5,000
Nine Spitfires = 40 Messerschmitts
Give as many penny units as you can afford

BUS MAINTENANCE

'THEY ALSO SERVE'

1

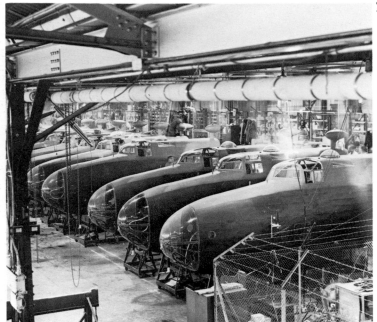

2

3

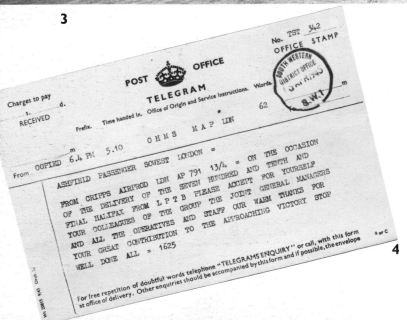

4

After experience gained in servicing Spitfires and Hurricanes in the summer of 1940, London Transport joined forces with four motor companies to manufacture Handley Page Halifax heavy bombers for the Ministry of Aircraft Production.

(1 & 2) Four thousand staff were involved in this work, which was carried out at Chiswick, Aldenham and Leavesden.

710 complete aircraft and enough spares to make 50 more were built between mid-1941 and April 1945.

(3) The last Halifax to be built by London Aircraft Productions was handed over to the RAF at a special ceremony at Leavesden.

(4) It was named *London Pride* by Lord Ashfield, who read out a congratulatory telegram from Stafford Cripps, the Minister of Aircraft Production, thanking all those who had taken part in the work.

Many other London Transport facilities were turned over to the war effort.

(5) In the safety of the newly completed Central Line tunnels between Leytonstone and Gants Hill, the Plessey Company manufactured aircraft components.

(6 & 7) 55 Green Line coaches were made available to the American Red Cross and converted for use as 'Clubmobiles' to serve the American Forces while they were in Britain.

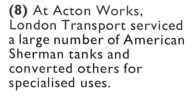

(8) At Acton Works, London Transport serviced a large number of American Sherman tanks and converted others for specialised uses.

The war with Germany ended on 8th May 1945 (Victory in Europe Day) and thousands of people celebrated on the streets of London. Six years of war had taken a considerable toll on London Transport:

22,580 members of staff were called to the armed forces, 122 receiving military decorations.

181 staff were killed on duty and 1867 seriously injured.

245 staff were killed off duty and 1006 injured.

166 buses, 60 trams, 15 trolleybuses and 19 railway cars were destroyed by enemy action.

CHAPTER
3
Post War Recovery
1945-1962

(Previous page) A poster by Molly Moss, 1950.

London had to wait a year to celebrate officially the end of the war in Europe. People had already endured nearly six years of disruption to their daily lives and the relief that it was now all over was tempered somewhat by the difficulties in getting back to normal. Not surprisingly, it was impossible for London Transport to reinstate services at their pre-war level as soon as the war ended. Many vehicles had been completely destroyed by enemy action, and hundreds more were either damaged or badly run down through lack of maintenance. New 'RT' type buses were ordered almost immediately, but the rate of delivery was slow, and by 1948 London Transport was having to withdraw old vehicles from service more quickly than new replacements could be introduced. As short-term solutions to the shortage, buses and coaches were hired from other operators and some newly delivered bus bodies were mounted on pre-war 'STL' chassis. By 1950 the position had improved, and post-war RTs made up 65 per cent of the double-deck fleet.

It had already been decided to use some of the new diesel buses instead of trolleybuses to complete the tram replacement programme. The running costs of buses and trolleybuses were similar at the time, but buses offered greater route flexibility and there was no longer a strong financial incentive to continue using the tramway electrical distribution network for trolleybuses, as much of it would soon need replacing. The surviving trams were withdrawn between 1950 and 1952 when, on the night of 5th/6th July, huge crowds turned out for an emotional farewell to a cheap and popular form of transport that had served Londoners well for more than eighty years.

(1) Two 'RT' type buses, part of London Transport's contribution to the Victory Parade, passing in front of the royal dais in the Mall, 10th June 1946.

Plans to resume the interrupted New Works Programme on the Underground were reviewed in the light of post-war financial difficulties. London Transport was authorised to proceed only with the unfinished eastern and western extensions of the Central Line, which were completed to Epping and West Ruislip respectively between 1946 and 1949. Beyond Epping the branch to Ongar remained steam worked until 1957, while at the western end of the line the planned extension from West Ruislip to Denham was not included in the final scheme. With the application of new Green Belt planning regulations, there seemed little likelihood of substantial passenger traffic on the proposed tube extension north of Edgware to Bushey Heath. The plans were abandoned in 1950, and it was decided to make the unfinished railway depot at Aldenham, which had been used to build aircraft during the war, the basis of a large new bus overhaul works. The bus fleet had more than doubled in size since the 1920s, when Chiswick Works was opened by the LGOC. By the 1950s it was essential to provide more spacious and better equipped facilities for the overhaul of the massive standardised post-war bus fleet. Conversion and extension work at Aldenham was completed in 1956.

2

(2) Trams at Westminster carry home the crowds after the official Victory Celebrations, 1946.

(3) Passenger carrying on London Transport reached a peak in the late 1940s. Here football fans queue for trolleybuses in Tottenham High Road after a Spurs home game at White Hart Lane in 1949.

3

By this time all the remaining unfinished railway works of the 1935–40 programme had also been dropped. Electrification of the Northern Line beyond Mill Hill East to Edgware was never carried out, and the tracks were eventually removed. The old LNER branch line from Finsbury Park to Alexandra Palace via Crouch End and Highgate had been partly prepared for tube services, with new colour light signalling, electricity sub-stations and most of the necessary cabling, by late 1939. An increasingly unreliable LNER, then British Railways, steam service survived until 1954, but the tube trains never came.

London Transport's inability to get Government financial backing for these new railway projects in the immediate post-war period reflected both the economic austerity of these years and the new administrative framework created in 1947. The Labour Party's landslide victory in the General Election of May 1945 was a prelude to the nationalisation of many key industries and public utilities over the next three years. On 1st January 1948 the British Transport Commission came into being to run the railways, canals, and certain road services. Within this body a new London Transport Executive was created to replace the LPTB, the Board's shareholders being compensated by the Government. Only three months earlier Lord Ashfield had retired, leaving Lord Latham, the former Leader of the LCC, to succeed him as Chairman in the new era. As just one division of the BTC, London Transport was not high on the Government's list for capital investment. Priority was given to other essential areas of the economy such as house building and electricity generation, while within the public transport field the needs of the badly run-down British Railways network took precedence.

Coincidentally, in the first year of nationalisation the number of passengers carried by London Transport reached a peak total of 4,675 million. From 1949 onwards passenger usage of the central area road services declined continuously, apart from a brief revival during Festival Year (1951). The reduction in off-peak leisure travel was particularly marked. 1948 saw record attendances at football matches in London, for example, followed by a steady drop throughout the fifties. Meanwhile television sets appeared in a growing number of homes, particularly after the introduction of a commercial channel in 1955, and kept more people at home during their leisure hours. Car ownership also increased rapidly once wartime petrol rationing for private motorists was finally ended in 1950. The number of cars licensed in the London area more than doubled over the next ten years, contributing further to the reduced patronage of the red buses and trolleybuses, and causing increasingly severe road congestion. The population of Greater London began to decline after the war, but just outside, in London Transport's country area, it grew steadily as people moved out to the new towns established beyond the Green Belt. Here, at least, there was a demand for new services and

REHABILITATION

23 railway stations, 15 bus garages and 12 trolleybus and tram depots had direct hits or suffered severe damage from enemy action. Replacements and repairs are in hand – but

IT TAKES **TIME**

(1) The immediate post-war years presented a number of operating difficulties for London Transport and a series of posters by Fred Taylor appeared in 1946 explaining the problems of rehabilitation.

(2) Green Line coaches which had been adapted for military purposes were restored to their former condition for the resumption of the full Green Line service in 1946.

Manufacturers took some time to resume full vehicle production and by late 1947 fewer than 200 new buses had been delivered.

(3 & 4) As a temporary solution vehicles and drivers were hired from other operators. These buses remained in the liveries of their owners, but were given London Transport bullseye devices on their radiator grilles.

the operating area was extended in January 1952 when the LTE took over some of Eastern National's bus services in Grays and Tilbury. Both the country bus and Green Line coach networks were considerably expanded and improved in the fifties and early sixties.

The London trolleybus fleet reached a peak total of 1,811 vehicles in 1952, making it the largest in the world, but oil was plentiful and diesel buses no more expensive to run. In 1954 London Transport unveiled its revolutionary new Routemaster bus. It could seat 64 passengers, but because it was constructed largely of lightweight aluminium alloy it weighed virtually the same as the 56-seat 'RT'. RM 1 was the first of a fleet designed to replace London's trolley-buses, and between 1954 and 1958 this bus and three other prototypes underwent extensive trials. When full-scale production of the 'RM' began in 1959 London Transport had a bus as sturdy and reliable as anything else on the road. By then, though, the long-term effects of the prolonged bus strike in the early summer of 1958 were being felt. During the 'busless' seven weeks of May and June people had been forced to find other means of getting around the capital. London buses had lost customers, and many were lost for ever. A number of routes were withdrawn, and services on others were reduced because of falling patronage. Staff shortages, first experienced by London Transport in the early 1950s, increased and a large number of surplus buses were withdrawn and sold.

The 'buses for trolleybuses' replacement programme began in March 1959, initially using surplus 'RT' family buses, but later new Routemasters. The last trolleybuses were withdrawn in May 1962, although with rather less ceremony than when the trams had been replaced ten years earlier. The London suburbs seemed strange without these silent, gliding, electric vehicles and the 'spiders' webs' of overhead wires, the removal of which transformed areas like Manor House, Stratford Broadway and Holloway. For the first time since the formation of London Transport, its entire fleet of road vehicles was diesel powered.

On the Underground the only major modernisation work for which expenditure was approved by the Government in the 1950s, concerned the outer sections of the Metropolitan Line. This, together with large orders for new rolling stock, the building of a new depot at Upminster, and the reconstruction of Notting Hill Gate station did much to improve the system by the early 1960s. The new trains for both tube and surface lines were built of aluminium alloy, which was left unpainted. This light, non-corrosive material was first used extensively in a batch of 'R' stock trains built for the District Line in the early 1950s, and from 1956 was used for all new Underground car bodies. The delivery of the new trains enabled much of the remaining pre-LPTB rolling stock to be withdrawn. The new fleet of 'A' stock trains for the Metropolitan Line displaced all the remaining Metropolitan Railway compartment stock, as well as the unique 1920s electric locomotives which bore the names of famous 'Metroland' residents, real and imaginary. The Metropolitan Line was transformed by 1962 into a modern suburban railway, with new trains, the provision of extra tracks between Harrow-on-the-Hill and Moor Park, and the electrification of the lines from Rickmansworth to Amersham and Chesham. No longer would passengers waiting on the stations between Finchley Road and Wembley Park be able to watch an 'up' Met express race past, hauled by *John Lyon* or *Sherlock Holmes*. The modernised Met was in keeping with the new Underground image of the sixties, soon to be further enhanced by the showpiece of the decade, the Victoria Line.

3

2

4

The loaned vehicles were all returned in 1950, by which time over 2,500 of the new AEC and Leyland 'RT' family buses were in service.

(5) This convoy of new RTs was photographed in January 1950 on its way to London from the Saunders Engineering coachworks in Anglesey.

5

Much of the preparatory work for the eastern extension of the Central Line had reached an advanced stage when construction was suspended because of the war.

(1) The subways leading to the booking hall at Gants Hill had been completed by 1939.

(2) In 1939–40 Loughton station was rebuilt by the LNER, prior to electrification for tube services.

(3) The new station, designed by Stanley Hall & Easton and Robertson, was an interesting departure from the established Holden style and featured curved concrete platform canopies.

(4) The surface building at Redbridge station, designed by Holden, was completed in 1947.

All the new stations featured fluorescent lighting, first tried out at Piccadilly Circus in 1945. Most of the trains required for the extension services were composed of 'standard' stock which had been displaced from the Northern and Bakerloo Lines by new trains in 1938–40 and stored in the open throughout the war, necessitating their complete refurbishment before re-entering service.

(5) A test train is seen here at Wanstead as finishing touches are made to the platform.

(6) Holden's unique barrel-vaulted platform concourse at Gants Hill was built in a majestic style reminiscent of the Moscow Metro.

The Central Line extensions were opened in stages between December 1946 and September 1949, more than trebling the route mileage of the line.

(*Main picture*) In the west the old Wood Lane station was replaced by a large new station named White City, opened in 1947.

(1) The design work by the Board's architect Thomas Bilbow, which included neat functional platform seating, won an award at the 1951 Festival of Britain.

Further west Central Line services were extended over new tracks beside the Great Western main line from North Acton to Greenford and West Ruislip in 1947–48.

(2) Four of the new stations on this section had distinctive 'butterfly-shell' reinforced concrete canopies.

(3) Tom Eckersley's 1948 poster announced the opening of the line in one direction to West Ruislip and in the other to Loughton.

(4) The final six mile section between Epping and Ongar, although part of the Central Line, remained steam-operated by British Railways until electrification was completed in November 1957.

2

3

4

I

Two major events, the 1948 Olympic Games and the 1951 Festival of Britain, helped to relieve the gloom of early post-war London at a time when rationing of many commodities was still in force. Britain hosted the Olympics in July and August 1948, with the principal events being held at Wembley Stadium.

(1) The 1948 Olympic Games attracted many visitors from the rest of Britain and overseas, who were guided to the events in the capital by a special London Transport map.

(2) Extra Underground services were provided to Wembley Park station which was enlarged to handle the crowds travelling to the Stadium.

(3) London Transport also provided most of the official transportation for athletes and officials.

The early 1950s saw a number of goodwill tours abroad by London Transport buses and staff.

(4) The first took place in 1950 when four new vehicles were sent on a 4000 mile tour of seven European countries to publicise the forthcoming Festival of Britain.

5

(5 & *main picture*) The main exhibition site for the Festival was on the South Bank, where London Transport displayed one of its new aluminium-bodied Underground cars.

(1) London Transport's programme of organised coach tours to places of interest in the capital was expanded in the early 1950s, one innovation being a combined road and river tour.

(2) The Thames was featured in this special 1951 double poster by John Minton.

The sightseeing excursions were the first services on which London Transport's new coaches were used. Experiments had been carried out since 1949 with underfloor-engined single-deck vehicles, and in 1951

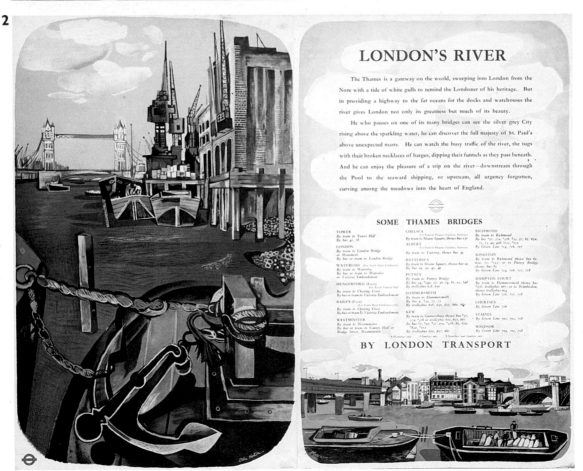

LONDON'S RIVER

The Thames is a gateway on the world, sweeping into London from the Nore with a tide of white gulls to remind the Londoner of his heritage. But in providing a highway to the far oceans for the docks and warehouses the river gives London not only its greatness but much of its beauty.

He who pauses on one of its many bridges can see the silver grey City rising above the sparkling water, he can discover the full majesty of St. Paul's above unexpected masts. He can watch the busy traffic of the river, the tugs with their broken necklaces of barges, dipping their funnels as they pass beneath. And he can enjoy the pleasure of a trip on the river—downstream through the Pool to the seaward shipping, or upstream, all urgency forgotten, curving among the meadows into the heart of England.

SOME THAMES BRIDGES

BY LONDON TRANSPORT

the first of an eventual 700 new buses, known as the 'RF' type, were built by AEC with bodywork by Metro-Cammell.

(3) The initial 25 to be delivered were 35-seat vehicles with glass roof panels for private hire work.

(4) These were followed immediately by a batch of 39-seat Green Line coaches.

(5) 15 wide-bodied coaches ('RFW' type) for luxury private hire were also added to the fleet in 1951.

4

5

3

(6) The whole range of tours available in Festival Year was advertised in a distinctive poster by Abram Games.

6

The tram replacement programme, which had been interrupted by the war, was resumed in 1950, using diesel buses instead of trolleybuses for the new services.

(1) Trams on six routes serving Battersea and Wandsworth ran for the last time on 30th September.

2

(2) They were replaced early next morning by new 'RT' type buses.

(3) The new vehicles had been stockpiled since delivery in a yard beside Edgware garage.

(4) For most of the redundant trams there was just one more destination —George Cohen's scrapyard at Charlton.

3

4

(1) In the final months of tram operation there were a number of special runs for enthusiasts, including a tour of the remaining system by car No. 1, the last tram built by the London County Council in 1932. This was one of several cars sold for further service to Leeds Corporation.

(2) The last two tram routes running out to north London through the Kingsway Subway were abandoned on 5th April 1952.

2

1

3

After the April conversion the only remaining tram routes were operated from Abbey Wood and New Cross depots in south-east London.

(3) At the end of June, posters appeared on the sides of all cars reminding Londoners that they had only one more week to take a ride on a tram.

(4) Souvenir tickets were issued for all journeys in the final week.

4

5

(5) In the early hours of 6th July, the last service tram arrived at New Cross depot surrounded by a large crowd of well-wishers.

(6) Shortly afterwards this car, 'E3' class No. 1951, met the same fate as most of London's trams.

6

1

2

3

4

In the late 1940s and early 1950s London Transport's bus fleet still contained many pre-war and non-standard wartime utility vehicles.

(1) This view of Regent Street shows two standard 'STL's (*left and right*) with a utility Daimler (*centre*), all still displaying wartime economy reduced destination blinds.

(2 & 3) Ticket issue also remained virtually unchanged, with Bell Punch machines being used on most services.
There was a different colour ticket for each fare value, and the tickets were punched against the appropriate destination

(4) The number and value of the tickets issued could be checked by counting the 'confetti' retained in the Bell Punch. '*A trick of nature has destined women for this job,*' commented London Transport Magazine, '*unlike men, they are practically never colour blind*'.

(5) By the time this photograph of Victoria bus station was taken in 1953, only four years after the Regent Street view opposite, the double-deck bus fleet had been considerably rationalised. All but one of the 18 buses seen here is of the post-war 'RT' family.

(6 & 7) A new roll-ticket machine, the Gibson, was introduced by London Transport in 1953 and over the next five years these replaced Bell Punches on all central area buses and trolleybuses.

5

6

7

Christmas in London has been brightened since 1947 by a giant tree in Trafalgar Square donated each season by the citizens of Oslo, Norway, as a gesture of thanks for British assistance during the Second World War.

(1) The fifth tree to arrive was featured in this 1951 London Transport poster by Maurice Wilson.

(2) The Christmas decorations in Regent Street first appeared in 1954 and soon became one of the seasonal sights of the capital, best viewed from the top of a London bus.

London Transport wishes you a Merry Christmas and a Happy New Year

1

2

4

5

The Coronation

(3) The Coronation of Queen Elizabeth II on 2nd June 1953 attracted large crowds of sightseers into the capital. London Transport provided full details of the many extra services in a pocket map and ran special Underground trains to convey 15,000 schoolchildren to the Embankment, where places were reserved for them to watch the procession.

(4) In all some 44,000 people used the bus services to and from the procession area on Coronation Day, and that evening Trafalgar Square was still jammed with buses carrying the crowds home. It is unlikely that London Transport will ever again mount such an elaborate one-day operation.

3

(5) A number of London Transport posters with a royal theme were produced in Coronation year, including this example designed by John Bainbridge.

A new programme of bus garage construction was instituted in the early 1950s.

(**1 & main picture**) The most impressive of the new buildings was Stockwell Garage, designed by Adie, Button and Partners, which at the time of its construction in 1951–52 boasted the largest expanse of roof without intermediate support anywhere in Europe.

(2) In September 1949 London Transport decided not to proceed with the proposed Northern Line extension from Edgware to Bushey Heath. The buildings at Aldenham which were to have formed the new Underground depot became available for conversion and enlargement into a bus overhaul works.

Construction began in 1952 and was completed in 1956.

(3) Aldenham Works was intended primarily to overhaul the fleet of post-war 'RT' buses, which had been designed with the maximum number of easily interchangeable parts, as well as provision for swopping complete bodies between chassis.

(4) Buses were sent to Aldenham every three or four years and followed a flow-line overhaul procedure, which included steam cleaning on the body inverter.

3

4

(1) In 1956 London Transport celebrated the centenary of the founding of the London General Omnibus Company with a parade of historic vehicles in Regents Park and a commemorative issue of the staff magazine.

(2) The same year saw the entry into public service of London Transport's revolutionary new bus, the Routemaster. RMI, the prototype, had been built in 1954 and extensively tested for two years before entering service on route 2. The Routemaster was designed as a replacement vehicle for the trolleybus fleet and featured a number of mechanical improvements including fully automatic gear change, power assisted steering and independent suspension. The bodywork was largely of lightweight aluminium construction.

(3) Three further 'RM' prototypes were built and tested before full production began, including a Green Line coach version (CRL4) which entered service in 1957.

Silver Trains

The first major advance in Underground rolling stock construction after the war was the introduction of non-corrosive lightweight aluminium alloy in the manufacture of bodywork and underframes. 90 new 'R' stock cars built for the District Line by Metro-Cammell were the first to be constructed in this way.

(4) Most of these were painted red, but one complete eight-car train, which entered service in January 1953, was left unpainted.

Operating experience with the 'silver' train led London Transport to adopt unpainted aluminium bodywork as standard for all future rolling stock.

(5 & 6) The first tube stock constructed in this way were three seven-car trains built in 1956, which were otherwise very similar in appearance to the 1938 stock. They entered service on the Piccadilly Line in 1957.

1

2

3

Although the population of Greater London began to decline after the war, it continued to increase in London Transport's country bus area.

(1) Some routes with low bridges were busy enough to justify the use of special 'low height' double-deckers. Between 1950 and 1952 London Transport took delivery of 76 new buses with low bridge bodies (RLH type), 52 of which were used on country services.

(2) When the new single deck 'RF' type became available in 1951, large numbers were allocated to the country area.

(3) Some lightly used routes, especially those that served remote villages, were operated by smaller pre-war vehicles, which were replaced in 1953 by 84 26-seat Guy 'GS' type single deckers.

New Town Services
Country bus services were expanded in the 1950s to serve the new towns of Crawley, Harlow, Hatfield/ Welwyn Garden City, Hemel Hempstead and Stevenage.

(4) The large number of buses allocated to run on the additional routes necessitated the building of several new garages, including one at Hatfield completed in 1959.

(5) Most of the new town services were operated with green 'RT' type double-deckers.

(6) Bus stations were an integral part of new town centre planning, as here at Stevenage.

4

5

6

The most serious difficulty facing London Transport in the 1950s was a shortage of bus operating staff.

(1) From 1951 the wartime policy of engaging women as conductors was resumed.

(2) Five years later London Transport began direct recruitment of new staff from Barbados. This helped, but did not solve, the problem, which was a contributory factor in the steady decline in red bus usage after 1952.

(3 & 4) Even more passengers were lost after the long strike in 1958 over busmen's pay. For seven weeks there were no familiar red buses in normally crowded thoroughfares such as Oxford Street.

(5) A few 'pirate' services were run by private operators during the strike.

(6) Attempts to promote off-peak travel had begun in 1956 with the introduction of Green (Country Bus) Rover tickets, to which Red (Central Bus) Rovers and Twin (Central Bus and Underground) Rovers were added in 1957 and 1958.

(7) After the strike the famous 'Hop on a Bus' slogan was coined and used for a two year publicity campaign, but the immediate effect of the industrial action was the withdrawal of many lesser used services and surplus vehicles.

5

6

7

Hop on a BUS

A street map showing fifteen selected Bus Routes which take you to all the places of interest in central London – together with an index and grid

LONDON TRANSPORT
55 BROADWAY SW1
ABBEY 1234

ROVER ROUND BY LONDON TRANSPORT

CENTRAL BUSES 5/-

UNDERGROUND 8/6
CENTRAL BUSES

COUNTRY BUSES 5/-

1

2

3

In contrast to the road services, passenger travel on the Underground remained at virtually the same level throughout the 1950s, with between 666 and 695 million journeys being made every year.

(1) Most of the rolling stock used in the 1950s was pre-war, such as this 1920 'F' stock train about to clear football crowds from Wembley Park after an International match between England and Scotland in April 1955.

(2) This driver's view of a Northern Line platform at Charing Cross station was taken during the rush hour in March 1959.

(3) In spite of efforts to encourage employers to stagger working hours, peak hour scenes, such as this at Charing Cross (Embankment) in May 1956, have changed little apart from the fashions.

4

Under Night Streets

London's Underground never sleeps. Every night after the last trains have run an army of staff carries out essential maintenance and other tasks. These scenes from the early 1950s show

(4) 'Fluffers' cleaning the tunnels.

(5) Ventilator duct sweeping.

(6) Advertisement posting.

(7) Rat catching, which at that time was carried out using ferrets.

5

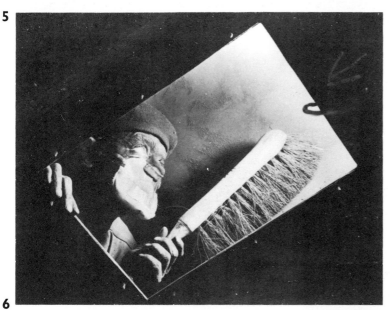

6

7

The London Trolleybus fleet reached a peak total of 1811 vehicles in 1952, making it the largest in the world.

(1) After the war the only new trolleybuses delivered were the wide-bodied 'QI' class vehicles built in 1948–52 at Ham, near Kingston, by British United Traction Ltd. These replaced the original LUT trolleybuses and vehicles destroyed during the war.

(2) The trolleybus network covered over 250 route miles. In some parts of London trolleybuses completely dominated the road transport scene, as in this view at Manor House in February 1955.

(3 & 4) When the replacement of the trolleybus system began four years later, it was generally the oldest vehicles that were withdrawn first, including the 'C3' class of 1936 (3), as well as non-standard vehicles such as the 'SA' class acquired during the war (4).

1

2

3

4

Buses for Trolleybuses

As early as 1949 the decision had been taken to replace all London's trolleybuses with diesel buses, but it was another ten years before the conversion programme got under way.

(5) Initially surplus 'RT' and 'RTL' type buses were used, but from late 1959 Routemasters, the larger new buses designed specially for trolleybus replacement, were introduced.

(6) The first conversion involving RMs took place on 11th November 1959, when they entered service at Poplar and West Ham garages.

5

6

(1) As conversions took place the overhead wires, and usually the traction poles as well, were removed. In this view at Moorgate in 1961, one of the first long-bodied 72-seat 'RML' Routemasters is seen operating on trolleybus replacement route 104. Once the conversions had begun, it took only three years to eliminate trolleybuses from London.

(2) Minor inconveniences such as dewirements disappeared with them. 'L3' class trolleybus No. 1521, shown here in Kingston shortly before the final conversion in 1962, was used for the last service run back to Fulwell depot on 8th May (*main picture*).

(3) This conversion appropriately covered most of the routes which had been operated by London's first trolleybuses in 1931, and early in the day the only surviving example of the original LUT fleet, then preserved in the Museum of British Transport at Clapham, was brought out for a special run. This vehicle is now on display in the London Transport Museum, Covent Garden.

(4) Most of the trolleybuses were scrapped at Colindale although many of the post-war vehicles had already been sold for further service in Spain.

3

4

The only major Underground modernisation for which expenditure was approved by the Government in the 1950s concerned the outer section of the Metropolitan Line.

(1) Joint working with British Railways trains out of Marylebone and the need to change from electric to steam haulage at Rickmansworth often caused congestion and delay on the Metropolitan Line. A £3.5 million improvement scheme, begun in the late 1950s, involved four-tracking of the line between Harrow-on-the-Hill and Moor Park, and electrifying beyond Rickmansworth to Amersham and Chesham. Both Northwood and Moor Park stations were rebuilt.

(2) All the old rolling stock on the Watford, Chesham and Amersham services was replaced between 1961 and 1962 with new aluminium 'A' (Amersham) stock.

(3 & 4) This led to the withdrawal from passenger service of the 'Metro-Vick' electric locomotives used on the Met's long distance services for nearly 40 years (3) and the 1920s 'T' stock multiple units (4).

(5 & 6) The new trains had spacious open saloons in contrast to the traditional compartments of the old Metropolitan Railway stock.

1

2

3

4

5

6

Notting Hill Gate station was extensively rebuilt in 1958–60 in connection with London County Council road improvement works.

(1) A new sub-surface ticket hall was constructed and improved interchange facilities were provided between the Central and Circle Lines.

(2) The new escalators were the first on London Transport to have aluminium panels. The overall style and predominantly grey and maroon colour scheme of the new station marked a complete departure from the established Holden pattern.

(3) A new £1 million rolling stock depot for the District Line, accommodating 34 trains, was opened at Upminster in December 1958.

(4) The following year full-scale production of new aluminium tube stock commenced. After delivery from the manufacturers, Metro-Cammell of Birmingham, the trains were prepared for service at Ruislip Depot.

(5) On 14th December 1959 the first of these trains entered service on the Piccadilly Line, and from July 1960 they were also used on the Central Line.

3

4

5

Keeping the bus and
Underground services
running reliably in severe
weather conditions is
always difficult.

(1, 2 & 3) The heavy
snowfalls during the
particularly severe winters
of 1962 and 1963 caused
many problems, but
services were maintained
wherever possible.

Problems and Progress
1963-1979

The traffic grows, and the Londoner's dependence on his public transport grows, too ⊖ New circumstances need new techniques, new methods ⊖ New automatically-driven trains for the Victoria Line ⊖ New buses for London's Red Arrow and flat-fare routes ⊖ New machines for automatic fare collection to save staff on road and rail ⊖ More station car parks ⊖ London Transport must change to keep pace with the constantly changing pattern of London on the move ⊖

(*Previous page*) A poster by William Fenton, 1969.

January 1st 1963, and the 'big freeze' tightened its grip on the country. Sub-zero temperatures and appalling travelling conditions were hardly the best circumstances for the third phase in London Transport's history to begin. At midnight on 31st December 1962 the London Transport Executive ended its 15 year existence and became the London Transport Board, an independent undertaking responsible directly to the Ministry of Transport. Little else changed. Fewer people were relying on public transport to take them where they wanted to go. The vicious circle which had begun in the fifties continued: car ownership, and in consequence traffic congestion, increased, making bus services less reliable, which in turn led more people to use their cars instead of public transport. Television had replaced the cinema as the principal form of entertainment leading to less evening patronage of the buses and Underground. Staff shortages, especially on the buses, increased further.

Despite these continuing problems there were some encouraging developments. More new buses and trains were entering service, and a completely new Underground line—the first for over fifty years—was in the making. The new railway was designed to link the West End with the main line rail termini at Victoria, Euston and King's Cross as well as penetrating territory new to the Underground in north-east London. Plans for several new tube lines had been drawn up in the late 1940s and it was one of these that emerged, following years of investigation and discussion, as the Victoria Line. London Transport favoured the line and emphasised the benefits to road conditions in north-east London which would be achieved by its construction. The Government, who held the purse-strings, took some convincing that the line would be a worthwhile proposition, but a pioneering cost benefit study strongly underlined the wider social advantages of the plan. Meanwhile London Transport's engineers were preparing detailed plans for the eventual construction of the line, which finally received Government sanction on 20th August 1962. The enormous task of building the Victoria Line began the following Spring.

(1) An experimental bus-only lane in Park Lane, 1968.

Londoners will remember the sixties for tower blocks, Carnaby Street fashions, England winning the World Cup at Wembley—and one-man buses. In September 1966 London Transport announced a bold formula to improve the reliability of bus services and reduce the effects of staff shortages. This was the Bus Reshaping Plan, the most important recommendations of which were the progressive single-manning of all London's buses and a radical route restructuring. By this time London Transport already had a number of new front-entrance buses, both double and single deck, running experimentally and was also trying out new types of bus service. Some outer suburban routes had been converted to one-man operation from 1964, to join the many already in existence in the country area, and in April 1966 an express route called 'Red Arrow' was introduced in central London using large capacity 'standee' single-deckers. In early 1968 the last of the 72-seat versions of the tried and trusted two-man, rear-entrance Route-master were delivered, thereby ending a design tradition which went back to the beginning of the motor bus. By the mid-sixties the Routemasters seemed rather outdated, and most other operators were buying front-entrance buses for their fleets, but subsequent events proved that London Transport was wise to continue with the acquisition of Routemasters for as long as it did. Its faith in the bus led to the construction of a front-entrance version in 1966 but this vehicle was destined to be a 'one-off', the last in a long line of buses designed by London Transport and purpose-built for London conditions.

The 1968 Transport Act was to steer future bus purchase policy in a different direction by authorising a government grant of 50 per cent towards the cost of new buses provided that the vehicles conformed to approved specifications. London Transport's hands were thus tied. A large fleet of AEC Merlin single-deck buses, basically similar to those purchased for the Red Arrow services, was ordered and used for the first of the major suburban one-man schemes intro-duced in the Walthamstow and Wood Green areas in Sep-tember 1968. For the Londoner who had been used to a conductor collecting his or her fare, the one-man buses took much getting used to. Naturally enough many teeth-ing troubles were experienced, but as the number of one-man bus routes increased, so people gradually began to accept the change, realising that in many cases, because of staff shortages, a one-man bus was the only alternative to having no bus service at all.

The rose amongst the thorns for London Transport in the 1960s was, without doubt, the Victoria Line. Built at a cost of £91 million, and opened in stages between 1968 and 1971, it was at the time the most advanced underground railway in the world. By October 1972, when the new station at Pimlico was opened, the line was carrying over a

(2) The new bus station at Walthamstow Central BR/Victoria Line station, 1968.

(3) An automatically driven train entering Seven Sisters station on the new Victoria Line, 1969.

2

3

quarter of a million people each weekday. It was a fitting prelude to a 'season' of new line construction recalling the pioneering spirit of the early 1900s. By the end of 1972 work was already under way on the £25 million extension of the Piccadilly Line to Heathrow Airport, and the Government had approved stage one of the Fleet Line, a new tube railway from Stanmore to Lewisham.

For most Londoners the first visible sign of work on the Victoria Line was the construction of the Oxford Circus 'umbrella' during the Bank Holiday weekend in August 1963. A ramp was built over the road junction to allow work to proceed on the new station booking hall below.

(1 & 2) The umbrella was installed in less than 65 hours between Saturday night and Tuesday morning when the Circus was reopened for traffic.

Meanwhile above ground things were not going too well. Staff shortages continued to affect bus service reliability in spite of a continuous programme of one-man conversions. Furthermore, mechanical problems were afflicting the new single-deck buses, which were basically 'off-the-peg' products not specifically designed to cope with London's gruelling stop-start traffic conditions. Breakdowns, combined with difficulties in obtaining supplies of spare parts from the manufacturers, led to a shortage of vehicles on a scale previously unknown on London buses. A large number of double-deck Daimler Fleetlines were purchased between 1970 and 1977, but these suffered from the same mechanical problems as their single-deck counterparts. Moreover staff shortages applied not only to bus crews, but to other grades as well, including maintenance staff. The shortages of staff and buses were accentuated by the third and probably most serious problem: traffic congestion. One effective solution to this was the 'bus only' lane. In 1970 there were only three bus lanes in London, but over the next five years the Greater London Council increased this number to more than a hundred. In some cases the lanes carried buses against the normal traffic flow, thereby maintaining a convenient two-way service on one-way streets. The GLC also placed restrictions on private and commercial traffic in some areas, notably along most of Oxford Street, and introduced numerous traffic management measures designed to give buses priority over other vehicles.

Useful though they were, bus lanes benefited bus movement over only relatively short distances. Recognising this, London Transport carried out experiments with computerised route control techniques, coupled with the use of two-way radios, both by route controllers and bus drivers. A common problem on suburban one-man bus services was passenger boarding delays. To reduce these several experiments involving pre-paid and 'multi-ride' tickets were carried out in the seventies, on both flat-fare and graduated fare routes. The introduction of bus passes and, at the instigation of the GLC, travel permits for the elderly, also helped to alleviate the problem.

On 1st January 1970, under the terms of the Transport (London) Act 1969, the Greater London Council took over the finance and broad policy control of London Transport. The GLC became the overall transportation authority for London with powers to appoint the Chairman and members of the new London Transport Executive. As part of their new involvement with London Transport, the GLC financed

1

2

a number of experimental bus services. In the autumn of 1972, four flat-fare minibus routes, using small capacity single-deck vehicles, were introduced. These ran in areas where there was insufficient demand to justify a conventional bus service. A progression of the mini-bus idea came with 'Dial-a-Bus' in 1974.

Air travel was the only mode of public transportation increasing its custom during this period and London's Heathrow Airport became the world's busiest. Plans to extend the Piccadilly Line to Heathrow received Government approval in November 1970, and the long awaited extension was finally opened in December 1977. Just over sixteen months later the first (and as it turned out, probably the last) stage of the Jubilee (Fleet) Line was opened between Charing Cross and Stanmore. With the opening of the Jubilee Line there ended almost 20 years of continuous tube railway construction. Rising costs—out of all proportion to those envisaged when the Fleet Line was originally planned—seemed set to keep all further plans for new tube construction firmly on the drawing board.

In 1979 it was time to celebrate. 150 years earlier, the first London bus—George Shillibeer's 'Omnibus'—had trundled from Paddington to the Bank. Whether Shillibeer could have envisaged the difficulties that his 20th century successors would face, we shall of course never know. At least by the end of 1979, with a new localised bus management structure, an improved staff position and the delivery of a fleet of new double and single deck buses far more reliable than anything purchased since the Routemaster, London Transport could enter the eighties with some optimism.

As work got under way on London's new tube, the centenary of the Underground was celebrated. In May 1963 an open day was held at Neasden Works where a special parade of historic and modern rolling stock took place.

(3) A former Metropolitan Railway 'E' class locomotive hauled a milk van and a rake of 'Ashbury' coaches, all dating from the 1890s.

(4) The latest 'A' stock was a total contrast to Met 'A' class steam loco No. 23, built in 1866, and now on display in the London Transport Museum, Covent Garden.

3

4

London Transport began tackling the growing problems of staff shortages and traffic congestion in various ways.

(1) One-man bus operation, which had been used effectively on some lightly used LT country area services since before the war, was gradually extended to the central bus area from 1964, starting with some outer suburban routes. In September 1966, London Transport published a bus reshaping plan which envisaged the eventual conversion of all routes to OMO to solve the manpower shortage.

The bus plan also highlighted the challenge to bus services posed by the private car.

(2) Between 1956 and 1966 the number of cars entering central London during the morning peak hours increased by 60 per cent. Private cars made up nearly 80 per cent of the road traffic, but carried only a third of the passengers.

(3) An ingenious poster of 1965 demonstrated how buses made far more efficient use of road space. The same point held true when London Transport reissued the poster eight years later.

(4) Recognising that the problems which disrupted bus services required sophisticated solutions, London Transport had been experimenting since 1957 with 'BESI', a Bus Electronic Scanning Indicator system. A network of roadside scanners transmitted the location of buses to a central control unit thereby facilitating more effective route regulation.

3

4

These vehicles are carrying...

69 people who could all...

be on this one bus ➡

First published 8 years ago. Still true today.

BOEING

The Green Line coach fleet was completely modernised in the 1960s.

(1) 68 Routemaster coaches (RMCs) went into service in 1962–3.

(2) 43 lengthened versions (RCLs) were added in 1965. These vehicles differed from standard Routemaster buses in having folding doors, fluorescent lighting, luggage racks, more comfortable seating and, in the case of the RCLs, more powerful engines.

(3) In 1965 14 new Reliance coaches (RCs) were added to the single-deck fleet.

(4) In 1966–7 175 remaining Green Line RFs were re-styled with new colour schemes and double headlamps.

(5) Modernised RFs from Reigate and St. Albans Garages were used to operate a new express Green Line service, the 727, introduced in May 1967. This linked the three airports at Luton, Heathrow and Gatwick and at nearly 74 miles was London Transport's longest route.

PAY AS YOU ENTER PLEASE

INE

THE NEW GREEN LINE COACH

This experimental coach is running every half hour on Route 705 between Sevenoaks and Windsor.

It has the following new features:

- Quieter and smoother ride
- More seats
- Luxury seats with footrests
- Adjustable air-conditioning for each passenger
- Wide-view windows
- Fluorescent lighting
- Luggage racks

Take a trip on it. If you have any comments please send them to the Public Relations Officer, London Transport, 55 Broadway, S.W.I.

1

2

The City of London Corporation's massive scheme to re-develop the bomb-damaged Barbican area began in the late 1950s. Part of the project involved the re-alignment of the LT Circle Line and adjacent BR tracks into a more direct path between Moorgate and Aldersgate (Barbican) stations.

(1) Contracts for the work were placed in 1963 and by July 1964 construction was well under way. The path of the new lines runs diagonally across this view looking towards Moorgate from Aldersgate.

(2 & 3) Nine months later the concrete covered way had been completed.

(4) By the end of the year trains were running over the new route. Rubber bearings were used in the construction of the concrete deck to lessen the effect of vibration on the new buildings later erected above, which include large blocks of flats as well as the Barbican Arts Centre.

By the mid-sixties many of Britain's bus operators were using front-entrance, rear-engined double-deckers.

(1) In 1965 London Transport purchased 50 72-seat Leyland Atlanteans for comparative trials against the 'RML' type, which had the same seating capacity.

(2) Eight similar Daimler Fleetlines were also delivered for use in the country area. At the time one-man operation of double-deckers was not permitted, but during off-peak periods the Fleetlines were used as OMO single-deckers (with the top deck roped off) as a cost-saving measure.

(3) A single front-entrance rear-engined version of the Routemaster (FRM I) incorporating 60 per cent of standard RM body parts was built in 1966 and entered trial service in June 1967. No further examples were built because the Government bus grant provision in the 1968 Transport Act favoured the purchase of existing tried and tested designs.

1

2

3

4

5

STARTING APRIL 18

ROUTE 500
VICTORIA STATION-
MARBLE ARCH

This is London's new limited-stop flat-fare bus service—specially designed buses with room for 48 standing and 25 seated, running every 3-4 minutes to clear quickly the rush-hour crowds over this short and heavily used route. Outside the rush hours the Red Arrows provide a circular service ideal for Oxford Street shoppers.

Go shopping by Red Arrow

Shoppers' Specials

There are now three Red Arrow Express bus routes to London's West End shops, from Victoria, Charing Cross and Waterloo. Fast frequent services from 09 30–15 30, Mondays to Fridays. Flat fare only 6d. (no children's fares).

ROUTE **500**
VICTORIA STATION–HYDE PARK CORNER– GROSVENOR SQUARE–OXFORD STREET– MARBLE ARCH.

ROUTE **506**
VICTORIA STATION–HYDE PARK CORNER– PICCADILLY CIRCUS.

ROUTE **505**
WATERLOO–STRAND–CHARING CROSS– TRAFALGAR SQUARE–REGENT STREET– OXFORD STREET–PORTMAN SQUARE

Please have your 6d. ready as you board

Look for this bus.......and this sign

6

7

Red Arrows

(4 & 5) An experimental flat-fare express bus route called the 'Red Arrow' was introduced in April 1966 between Victoria and Marble Arch using new AEC Merlin single-deckers.

(6) The success of this service led to the creation of a network of nine Red Arrow routes in 1968, linking main line railway termini with the central shopping and business districts.

(7) To move as many passengers as possible over short distances, the Red Arrow buses were designed as 'standee' vehicles with a limited number of seats.

By 1965 work on the Victoria Line was well advanced. Wherever possible passenger inter-change with other lines had to be on the same level, and to arrange this at Finsbury Park it was necessary to re-align the southbound Piccadilly Line into a new tunnel. This was achieved with the minimum of service disruption by gradually enlarging part of the existing tunnel.

(1) The last train ran through the old tunnel at 00.03 on Sunday, 3rd October, 1965.

(2) New track was then installed overnight to link up with the new tunnel at a slightly lower level.

(3) Services were resumed at 14.08 that afternoon. The old tunnel can be seen on the left.

(4) Most of the running tunnels were excavated using mechanical rotary 'drum digger' shields. For the larger station tunnels traditional Greathead shields were used, behind which the clay was dug out with power-driven hand tools. As the shield was jacked forward a tunnel lining of cast iron or concrete segments was installed.

(5) At the stations, an inner 'skin' of brick and plaster walls and corrugated iron panels for suspended false ceilings were added.

(6) While the Victoria Line was being built, experiments with automatic train operation were carried out on the Hainault to Woodford section of the Central Line using converted 1960 tube stock. As a result of these successful trials London Transport decided to use an automatic train operating system for the new line.

4

5

6

TILE MOTIFS ON THE VICTORIA LINE

by Julia Black
An adaptation of a William Morris design. He was born and worked for a time in Walthamstow where a museum displays examples of his work.

by Hans Unger
The black horse also appears as a sculpture, by David McFall, on the exterior of the station.

by Edward Bawden
The name is derived from a ferry over the river Lea in earlier times. The word 'hale' is said to be a corruption of 'haul'; or perhaps 'hail'.

by Hans Unger
The seven sisters were seven trees which gave a name to the locality.

by Tom Eckersley
The crossed pistols refer to the duelling that took place here when this was outside the edge of London.

by Edward Bawden
The high bury, manor or castle, was destroyed at the time of the Peasants' Revolt (1381).

by Tom Eckersley
A literal design based on a cross and crowns. The King concerned (if there ever was one) is not identified.

by Tom Eckersley
A reminder of the Doric Arch which stood on the station site.

by Crosby/Fletcher/Forbes
A maze or Warren as a pun on the name. A solution is possible for the traveller with time to spare.

by Hans Unger
A device to incorporate the circle of the circus with the linking of the Bakerloo, Central and Victoria Lines.

by Hans Unger
A bird's eye view of the trees in the park against the green background of the grass.

by Edward Bawden
The great Queen herself, from a silhouette by Benjamin Pearce. A plaque in the ticket hall records the visit of Queen Elizabeth to open the Victoria Line in March 1969.

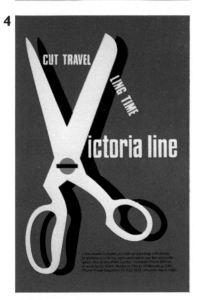

(1) The colour scheme used throughout the Victoria Line was predominantly grey, blue and white, but an element of individuality was given to the stations by incorporating tile motifs by different artists. Each design was related to the station name.

The Victoria Line was opened in stages. On 1st September 1968 trains began running between Walthamstow Central and Highbury & Islington. Exactly three months later services were extended to Warren Street.

(2 & 3) The official opening through to Victoria was performed by Her Majesty the Queen on 7th March 1969. This was her first trip on an Underground train since the age of 13, and the first time since 1850 that a reigning monarch had opened a railway line in Britain.

(4) The new line cut journey times across central London drastically: Victoria to King's Cross, for example, which had previously taken 24 minutes with a change, was reduced to 10 minutes. By the end of 1969 1.25 million passengers a week were using the Victoria Line.

(1) With a view to improving the efficiency and economy of fare collection on the Underground, London Transport installed automatic entrance gates at three stations in 1964. These gates opened only when a passenger inserted a magnetically coded ticket.

(2) After two years of trials it was decided to use a similar system at all the new Victoria Line stations then under construction. The Victoria Line opened with automatic fare collection throughout, but AFC methods have been progressively improved and modified ever since.

The most important innovation on the Victoria Line was automatic train control, based on a safety signalling and driving command system.

(3) The controls of each train on the Victoria Line respond to coded electrical impulses in the running rails. These are detected by equipment mounted underneath the front of the train.

(4 & 5) Braking and acceleration are automatic. The train operator can over-ride this system, but in normal operation he acts as the guard, opening and closing the train doors at stations, then pushing the start buttons for the automatic system to take over. He is also in direct phone contact with a central control room at Cobourg Street near Euston.

In 1965 it was decided to extend the route by 3.5 miles south of Victoria to Brixton. This was the first tube line to be built south of the river since the Morden extension of the Northern Line was completed in 1926.

(1) Originally there were to be only two intermediate stations, at Vauxhall and Stockwell, which provided interchange facilities with BR and the Northern Line respectively. In 1969 an additional station at Pimlico was authorised.

(2, 3 & 4) The Brixton extension was opened by Princess Alexandra on 23rd July 1971.

(5) Pimlico station, which provided convenient Underground access to the Tate Gallery for the first time, was not completed until September 1972.

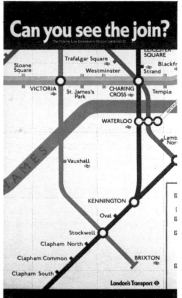

3

4

Rather surprisingly, steam locomotives on London Transport's completely electrified system outlived those on British Railways by three years. 11 small tank engines inherited in 1933 from the Metropolitan and District Railways were maintained until the late 1950s for use on engineers' trains and general non-passenger duties. Between 1957 and 1963 these ageing locomotives were replaced by a fleet of ex-Great Western pannier tanks purchased from British Railways.

(1, 2 & 3) By 1971 only three of the panniers survived, and when these were withdrawn on 6th June a special commemorative run was made between Barbican and Neasden.

New Trains for the Circle

As the Metropolitan was saying farewell to its links with steam a new fleet of trains was being introduced on the busy Circle and Hammersmith & City services.

(4, 5 & 6) 212 'C' (Circle) stock cars were ordered in 1968 from Metro-Cammell and delivered from mid-1970 onwards. To reduce boarding and alighting times on the Circle Line service, where most passengers only travel for short distances and there is constant inter-change, the new trains were designed with four sets of double doors on each side. A further batch was delivered in 1977 for use on the Edgware Road section of the District Line.

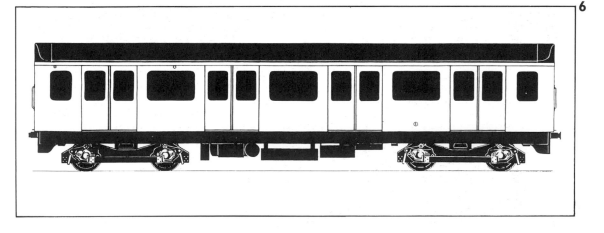

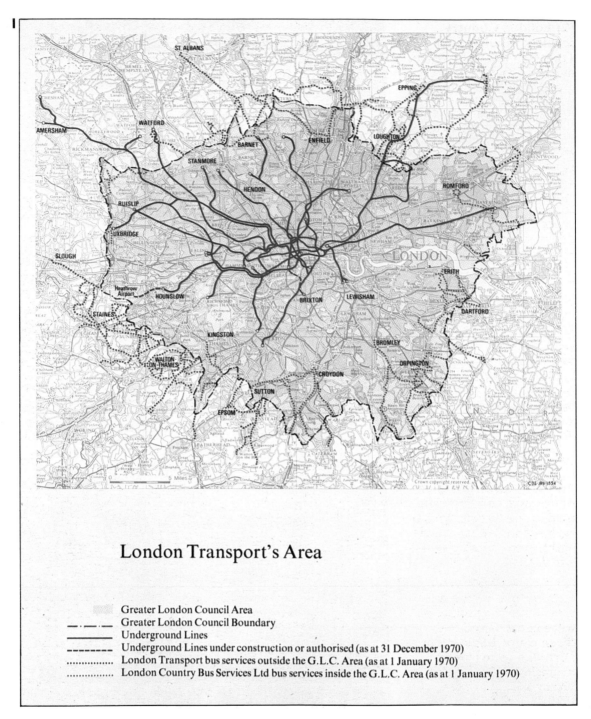

London Transport's Area

Greater London Council Area
Greater London Council Boundary
Underground Lines
Underground Lines under construction or authorised (as at 31 December 1970)
London Transport bus services outside the G.L.C. Area (as at 1 January 1970)
London Country Bus Services Ltd bus services inside the G.L.C. Area (as at 1 January 1970)

From 1st January 1970 financial and broad policy control of London Transport was transferred to the Greater London Council under the terms of the Transport (London) Act 1969. At the same time ownership of LT's Green Line and Country Bus services was handed over to the National Bus Company and given the new title London Country Bus Services Ltd.

(1) London Transport's operating area was thereby considerably reduced, largely to the GLC area.

(2) London Country acquired all of London Transport's former green bus and coach fleet, the most modern examples of which were 108 one-man operated AEC Merlin single-deckers delivered in 1967–8.

(3) By the time the GLC assumed responsibility for London Transport the conversion of suburban bus routes to one-man operation was well under way. Some of the early schemes involved the creation of networks of local 'flat-fare' services, initially in Walthamstow, Wood Green and Ealing (shown here).

The flat-fare routes were identified by a letter prefix to the number. On most of the new OMO services new AEC Merlin single-deckers were used.

(4) Those on the flat-fare routes were two-door 'standee' buses, while on the graduated fare services, such as the 242 shown here at Waltham Abbey, single-entrance/exit vehicles were used.

(5) To give improved weather protection for waiting passengers, roofs were constructed over three major bus stations at Turnpike Lane (1968), Hounslow (1970) and Victoria (shown here, 1970).

2

3

4

5

(1) Bus only lanes, which reduce delays caused by traffic congestion, were first introduced in 1968. The number increased considerably during the 1970s, and included the contra-flow lane in Piccadilly, which came into use in April 1973.

(2) Two-way radio communication between bus drivers and controllers was in use on seven routes by 1973, on six of them in conjunction with the Bus Electronic Scanning Indicator system. Radios were installed on all London's buses during the late seventies and early eighties, enabling crews to report unusual traffic conditions and to summon assistance in an emergency.

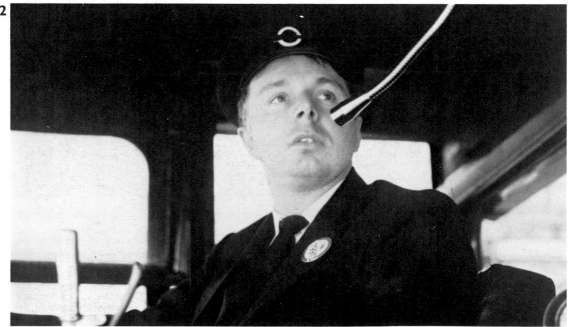

3

(3) From 1971 onwards bus radios were progressively issued to traffic inspectors to assist in route control.

(4) In 1973 CARLA (Computer Assisted Radio Location Aid) was introduced experimentally on route 11, one of central London's busiest services. A computer analysed coded signals from each bus on the service giving its whereabouts. This information was displayed in the form of a route diagram on a television screen in the Central Control Room. The controller could see the position of each bus and contact traffic inspectors to make adjustments to the running of buses where necessary.

4

1

2

This is a bus.
But think of it as a phone box.

In a phone box you must pay with the correct coins. Because it doesn't give change. So it should be with one-man buses. That way it goes a whole lot faster. Because giving change takes time. So if you think of it as a phone box and have the exact fare ready, you'll get through without hangups.

London's Transport. ⊖

We're not impressed by big money.

Please have your exact fare ready. Please.

London's Transport ⊖

(1) The operation of one-man double-deckers was made possible by new regulations in 1968. However, by this time London Transport had ordered a large number of new single-deck buses, including the first of an eventual 838 AEC Swifts (SMS type) which were short wheel base versions of the Merlin. After trials with the 'XA' and 'XF' type buses more double-deck Daimler Fleetlines were ordered for comparison with the single-deckers.

(2 & 3) The first of the new double-deckers (DMS type) went into service on routes 95 and 220 in January 1971. Eventually 2,646 Fleetlines were delivered, the last vehicles arriving in 1978.

(4 & 5) One man operation made better use of available staff resources, but on busy routes it was soon found to cause boarding delays, particularly when passengers did not have the correct money ready or experienced problems with the automatic ticket machines. An extensive publicity campaign in 1971 encouraged passengers to tender the right money.

1

(1 & 2) When more reliable automatic fare collection machines were installed in one-man buses from 1972 onwards, a further campaign was launched to persuade passengers to make use of the equipment, rather than pay their fares to the driver. Unfortunately the campaign had little effect, and in the late 1970s all AFC equipment was taken out of service. A number of experiments were carried out with pre-paid tickets and ticket strips, on which passengers cancelled a unit for each journey they made. As an inducement to purchase, the ticket strips were slightly cheaper than the normal fare.

(3) Initially the pre-paid, 'multi-ride' tockets were available only on flat-fare routes, but in 1978 bus routes in the Havering area were chosen for an experiment to assess the effect of making the tickets available on graduated fare services. The multi-ride fares were replaced in 1980 when flat-fare experiments were conducted in Havering and Harrow.

2

3

(4) Maintenance problems, particularly with the new buses used on one-man services contributed, along with traffic congestion and staff shortages, to serious bus service unreliability during the mid-1970s. The situation was made worse by disruptions to the flow of essential spare parts from component manufacturers. At one stage buses and coaches were hired from other operators to help ease the vehicle shortage, and some LT buses were 'cannibalised' to keep others on the road.

(5) In 1974 new government legislation gave women the opportunity to occupy jobs which formerly had been done exclusively by male staff. By 1975 LT had twenty women drivers and eight women inspectors on its books. By the end of the seventies there were women guards and train drivers too.

4

5

(1–4) The red double-decker bus was already a London institution in 1933 and there have been only a few changes to the basic livery since then. In 1969, as a commercial advertising experiment, a Routemaster was repainted to become an all-over advertisement for Silexine paints. From 1970 London Transport decided to offer advertisers all-over space on a limited number of vehicles, but there was a distinctly mixed public reaction to the 29 multi-coloured buses which subsequently appeared on the streets over the next seven years.

(5 & 6) The idea of buses 'sponsored' by advertisers was continued in 1977 when 25 Routemasters were repainted in an appropriate colour for the Queen's Silver Jubilee. A special feature of these buses was the addition of carpeting supplied by the wool industry.

1

2

3

4

(7) Two years later London Transport marked the 150th anniversary of the introduction of buses to the capital by painting 13 sponsored buses in a livery based on the colour scheme of George Shillibeer's 1829 Omnibus.

(8) A circular bus route called 'Shoplinker', serving the main West End and Knightsbridge shopping streets, was introduced in April 1979. The buses used on this service were given a distinctive red and yellow livery and fitted with audio equipment advertising the particular store which had sponsored the vehicle. Unfortunately Shoplinker was not a success and was withdrawn after only five months operation.

5

6

7

8

1

2

3

After years of discussion and planning, work on the three and a half mile extension of the Piccadilly Line from Hounslow West to London's Heathrow Airport began in April 1971.

(1) Part of the route was constructed beneath the Great West Road by the 'cut and cover' method, which involved digging a trench to accommodate the tracks, inserting side walls of interlocking concrete piles and roofing them over again at ground level before reinstating the road surface.

(2 & 3) Inside the airport perimeter, where the line passed under runways, the tunnels had to be drilled out at a deeper level. These photographs show the cross-over tunnel near Heathrow Central station under construction, and the tunnel shield and beam cutter after breaking through.

(4) The intermediate station at Hatton Cross, which serves the airport's engineering and maintenance areas, was opened on 19th July 1975.

(5) At platform level a mosaic design based on the old Imperial Airways 'speedbird' motif was incorporated on the support pillars.

1

(1) In preparation for the Heathrow extension the Piccadilly Line was re-equipped with a fleet of 87 new six-car trains known as 1973 tube stock, the first of which entered service in July 1975. Each car was six feet longer than normal tube stock and incorporated additional luggage space in the door recesses for airline passengers.

(2) The new station at Heathrow Central was equipped with a number of special facilities to help visitors arriving at the airport. Moving walkways link the station with the

UNDERGROUND EXTENSION TO HEATHROW 16 DECEMBER 1977

3

Fly the Tube

Take the Piccadilly Line to Heathrow Airport.
It's the only way to fly.

4

three existing air terminals and on the station concourse there are travel and tourist enquiry desks, a bureau de change and a passenger route indicator for the Underground, displaying information in English, French and German. Heathrow was also the first station on the London Underground to be fully equipped with internationally accepted pictogram signs.

(3) The Heathrow extension was opened by Her Majesty the Queen on 16th December 1977.

(4) People needed little encouragement to 'Fly the Tube'. In its first full year of operation eight million passengers used the Heathrow extension.

(1) The success of the four experimental minibus services introduced in 1972, using 16-seat Ford Transit vehicles, led the GLC to subsidise a further experiment in 1974 called 'Dial-a-Bus' linking Hampstead Garden Suburb with Golders Green Underground station. Intending passengers could hail the bus anywhere in the Suburb or telephone a controller at Golders Green who would arrange for the next bus to pick them up at, or near, their homes. Once demand patterns had been established 'Dial-a-Bus' was replaced in 1976 by a minibus service running on a fixed route.

All other new bus types ordered during the 1970s were 'off the peg' chassis designs. These were standard production models available to operators all over the country, and only a few modifications were made to London Transport's specifications before buses went into service.

(2) In 1976–77, 112 small Bristol single-deckers (seventeen 26-seat 'BS' types and ninety-five 39-seat 'BL' types) were delivered to replace some of the ageing 'RF' vehicles on suburban routes.

1

2

(3) The standard single-deck bus introduced throughout Britain in the 1970s was the Leyland National. After satisfactory trials with six vehicles in 1973, London Transport took delivery of a further 500 'LS' types between 1975 and 1981, including 69 Leyland National Mark IIs for use on Red Arrow services.

(4) 164 Metropolitan double-deckers ('MD' type) built by Metro-Cammell-Weymann on Swedish Scania Vabis running units were delivered in 1975/77.

3

4

An all-British version of the Metropolitan double-decker, with a Gardner engine, was developed by Metro-Cammell-Weymann and launched as the 'Metrobus' in 1977. Meanwhile Leyland had also been experimenting with a new double-deck design, code-named the B15. London Transport tested the prototypes of both designs and as a result placed large orders for both Metrobuses and 'Titans' (as the production B15s were named).

(1) The first production Titans entered service in December 1978 at Hornchurch Garage. Initially the 'T' types were confined to routes in north-east London.

(2) The following March the first of the main batch of Metrobuses began running from Fulwell Garage. They soon became a familiar sight on suburban routes throughout north and west London.

(*Main picture*) By the end of 1982, 805 new Metrobuses and 650 Leyland Titans were in service, replacing the less reliable Fleetlines.

(3) The first 250 Titans were the last buses with bodywork by Park Royal Vehicles, a company which had been building London buses for over 50 years by the time their west London coach works was closed in 1980. As the new buses were entering service, hundreds of enthusiasts turned out to photograph the last of the famous 'RT' type buses, which were withdrawn at Barking Garage in April 1979.

2

3

As part of a major new drive to increase efficiency London Transport's bus management was decentralised into eight

WATLING

Barnet

Mill Hill

Harrow

Cricklewood

Hampste

Uxbridge

ABB

Acton

Shepherds Bush

Victori

CARDINAL

Barnes

Putney

Cl

Wimbledon

Kingston

WA

operational districts in 1979. Under the new arrangements each area is under the control of a District General Manager who is responsible for the planning and operation of

LONDON BUSES
WATLING DISTRICT

LONDON BUSES
ABBEY DISTRICT

LONDON BUSES
CARDINAL DISTRICT

LONDON BUSES
WANDLE DISTRICT

between 25 and 30 bus routes as well as buses and staff at between seven and ten garages. Local identity plays an important part in the new structure, and the eight districts each have a

FOREST

Romford

Barking

Newham

Woolwich

SELKENT

name and a symbol appropriate to their locality. The symbols appear prominently on all buses, premises and printed material connected with each district.

Walthamstow

TOWER

Bank

Peckham

Penge

Bromley

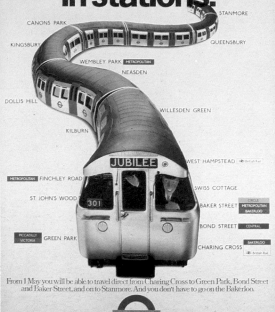

The 1949 London Plan Working Party Report, which had proposed the Victoria Line, also recommended the construction of another new cross-town tube. This became known as the Fleet Line, financial approval for which was granted by the Government in 1971. Construction began the following year and was

well advanced by 1977, when the name was changed to the Jubilee Line to mark the Queen's Silver Jubilee that year.

(1) Stage One consisted of a new line between Charing Cross and Baker Street, where it joined the existing Stanmore branch of the Bakerloo Line.

(2 & *main picture*) Bright colour schemes and sound absorbent materials were used in the new stations.

(3) In the dramatic new booking hall at Charing Cross, blue, green and yellow moulded plastics were employed in the design of the ticket office, collectors' booths and shop units.

The new Charing Cross station incorporated the former Strand (Northern Line) and Trafalgar Square (Bakerloo Line) stations as well as the new Jubilee Line platforms.

(1 & 2) A specially commissioned mural design by David Gentleman runs the entire length of both the Northern Line platforms. It depicts the construction nearby of the original memorial cross to Queen Eleanor built by King Edward I in 1291–94. The present Charing Cross standing immediately above the Underground booking hall is a Victorian replica.

3

4

(3) More recent, but fictional, events are portrayed in a series of decorative panels by Robin Jacques on the Jubilee Line platforms at Baker Street. These illustrate dramatic scenes from the adventures of Baker Street's most famous 'resident', Sherlock Holmes, including *The Hound of the Baskervilles*.

(4) The Jubilee Line was officially opened on 30th April 1979 by HRH The Prince of Wales, who later travelled the length of the line to Stanmore, riding in the driving cab for most of the journey. The train, like all others on the Jubilee Line, was composed of 1972 Mark II tube stock.

1

2

3

(1) London's first omnibus service was introduced between Paddington and the Bank on 4th July 1829 by George Shillibeer. The 150th anniversary of this occasion was celebrated by London Transport with several special events, including a parade of historic vehicles in Hyde Park and a horse bus service which ran during the summer months between Baker Street and the London Zoo in Regent's Park.

(2 & 3) At the annual Easter Parade in Battersea Park a procession of London buses representing the 150 years ranged from a replica of Shillibeer's first omnibus to one of the latest Metrobuses. The Shillibeer omnibus was built for the 100th anniversary celebrations in 1929, and in 1979 had just been beautifully restored for inclusion in the new London Transport Museum at Covent Garden, where it is now on permanent display.

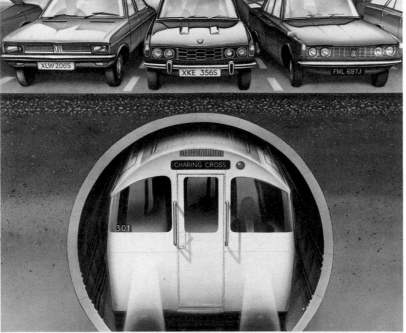

(*Previous page*) Poster by Foote, Cone & Belding, 1979

One factor above all others seems set to dominate the world of public transport for the forseeable future: finance. The role of transport during the present decade and beyond is now a matter of almost constant public debate, and some issues are always to the fore: how much will it cost, how much is to be invested and, above all, who is going to pay for it? London Transport will not be immune from the controversy which, if recent events are any indication, is bound to continue.

Nevertheless, there were some encouraging developments for London Transport at the start of the 1980s. Significant improvements in bus service quality, due in no small measure to the management changes introduced in 1979, have been achieved. Vehicle reliability has been improved, helped by a fleet of new double-deck Metrobuses and Titans, which have become a familiar sight on London's streets. Further improvement came in 1981 with the opening of three completely new bus garages in addition to those extensively rebuilt in the continuing programme of garage modernisation begun in the seventies. Some parts of the Underground are also being updated. A fleet of new trains was built for the District Line between 1980 and 1982, and new trains were ordered for the Jubilee Line for delivery in 1983, to enable the last of the 1938 stock cars to be withdrawn. Station improvement schemes are under way throughout the system, notably at Charing Cross (Bakerloo Line), and on the Central Line at Tottenham Court Road, Oxford Circus and Bond Street. Work has also begun on specifications for a fully automatic control system for the Central Line which will require new rolling stock in the 1990s.

The computer will be playing a more prominent role on London Transport during the coming years, both above and below ground. A new platform information system has been designed following successful trials at St James's Park station. The equipment consists of a matrix of light-emitting diodes, which can be illuminated to show any combination of words or figures and even diagrams. This makes it possible to display a variety of information to waiting passengers, including the destination, current location and arrival times of the first and subsequent trains. Drawing on the valuable experience gained with the BESI and CARLA route control systems in reducing the effect of traffic delays on buses, a new and more sophisticated computerised system called BUSCO (Bus Communications and Control) has been developed. This relays to the route regulators accurate bus schedule and location information, and gives them the facility to pass information and instructions to individual buses. BUSCO will initially be tested on a group of busy central London services.

Throughout the last twenty-five years, the period when operating problems have been most acute, London Transport has been very conscious that the standard of service

(1) The GLC 'Fares Fair' scheme of 1981 led to a major legal and political controversy. This leaflet was produced by the Council to defend its policy on fares.

provided has on occasions fallen below that which passengers expect. Some of the main problems, their causes, effects and remedies have already been discussed, but there are further external factors which direct policy and influence decisions. The future of London Transport will be determined in large part by political decisions both at County Hall and at Westminster. Such considerations have already had an effect on London Transport services operating across the Greater London boundary into the surrounding counties. Even after the country bus network became part of the National Bus Company in 1970 there were still a number of London Transport's familiar red buses running out to places like St. Albans, Leatherhead and Brentwood—now there are none. The 1972 Local Government Act placed a statutory duty on county councils to pursue policies for the coordination of public transport, with associated powers of finance for loss making services. Reduced public spending has caused many local authorities to cut their transport grants, the end result often being the withdrawal of services and the charging of higher fares on the sections which remain. Many London Transport services outside Greater London have been taken over by other operators, notably London Country. This process has continued into the eighties and has begun to affect the Underground. The Epping to Ongar section of the Central Line, which is outside the Greater London Council area, was reduced to a peak hours only service in December 1982, and Blake Hall station has been closed, because London Transport was not receiving a subsidy from Essex County Council to finance the line.

As one small part of the Underground contracts, so another expands. The Piccadilly Line Heathrow extension has been an undoubted success since it opened in 1977 and is now

(2) Two new express services called 'Airbus' were introduced in November 1980 between Heathrow and central London.

to be extended in a loop to serve the new Terminal 4. Westbound trains will leave Hatton Cross and use a new single track tube tunnel to the new station at Terminal 4 being built by the British Airports Authority. From there trains will run on under the Cargo Terminal and runways to the present Heathrow Central station before returning via existing tunnels to Hatton Cross and London. Work on the tunnel was set to begin during 1983.

There is little doubt that the new section of Piccadilly Line will be well used, but what of the rest of the Underground system and the buses? London Transport's position since the 1950s, like most urban public transport authorities, has been one of a declining number of passengers (particularly on the buses) and rising costs. It is no longer possible for such a system to be self-financing in the way that it was envisaged London Transport would be when it was created in 1933. On the other hand, it is neither practical nor desirable to leave city transport to private cars, which are an inefficient means of moving large numbers of people over relatively short distances. But if there are sound social and economic reasons for maintaining a public transport network, how is it to be paid for? The question of subsidy lies at the heart of the current debate about public transport. In early 1981 only 29 per cent of London Transport's costs were met by central government and GLC grants, the remainder having to come from passenger fares. The public transport systems in most of the world's major cities receive far higher grants, which enable them to keep the fares at much lower levels. In Paris the 1981 subsidy was 52 per cent, in Brussels 66 per cent and in New York 70 per cent.

In October 1981, at the request of the GLC, a controversial reduced fares scheme was introduced by London Transport under the banner 'Fares Fair'. It was hoped that greater use of public transport would be encouraged by a 33 per cent cut in fares to be held for four years. Road congestion would thereby be reduced and the environment enhanced: a worthy aim, but fierce controversy immediately arose over the cost to ratepayers. The supplementary rate demand which financed the cheaper fares was declared illegal by the House of Lords following an action by the London Borough of Bromley. The Law Lords emphasised that, under their

(1) 75 new trains for the District Line were ordered in 1977 and built over the next five years at Metro-Cammell's workshops in Birmingham.

(2) The 'D' (District) stock was built to replace the pre-war 'CO/CP' stock trains and the post-war 'R' stock. The new trains entered passenger service from January 1980 onwards.

3

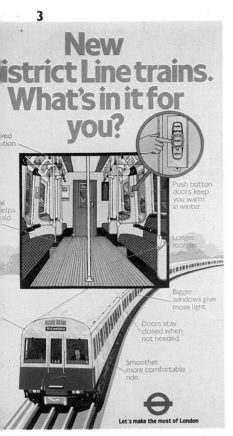

(3) The various new features of the trains, which include passenger operated doors, were explained in a poster at the time of their introduction.

interpretation of the Transport (London) Act 1969, London Transport must plan, so far as is practicable, to break even. The ending of 'Fares Fair' in March 1982 required a doubling of fares to meet London Transport's financial remit as the Courts seemed to be interpreting it. The related questions of fares, financial support and their effect on demand (and therefore service levels) will recur again and again in the coming years, but the sudden reversal of policy did little to establish a firm financial basis on which London Transport could plan for the eighties and beyond.

The development of London's transport over much of the last 150 years has been closely linked to the growth of the city. As London expanded, so did its public transport system, geared to meeting the changing needs of the new areas it served. A variation on this process is taking place in the 1980s. For many years the London Docks have been in decline, but work is under way to revitalise the entire Docklands area, creating new industries and employment opportunities. Good transport links are vital to such an area, and the favoured cheaper alternative to extending the Jubilee Line eastwards is to build a seven mile light railway link from the City to the Isle of Dogs, with a two and a half mile branch from Poplar to Mile End. Modern single-deck trams are proposed for this rapid transit system, which will run mainly on disused railway viaducts and freight lines.

So, more than thirty years after it bade farewell to London, the tram seems set to stage a comeback—just one of a number of important plans for the eighties which will breathe new life into London's public transport system. The period before 1990, with no major rolling stock replacement programme in the offing, presents an excellent opportunity to undertake an enhanced programme of capital investment projects for the Underground. If the necessary finance were made available, London Transport would carry out major modernisation schemes involving stations, signalling, track and power supply, as well as further developments of advanced train identification and communication systems. The fuel shortages of the mid-1970s brought home to many people the fact that public transport still has an important part to play in the daily life of London. There is at the moment a powerful public transport lobby and growing support for a more closely integrated transport system for the capital, to include not only London Transport services but also the British Rail network.

We have looked back over the first fifty years of one of the world's greatest public transport systems. There have been problems and there have been triumphs; there are fresh challenges and opportunities ahead. There is a will to succeed but London Transport will need the support of the policy makers, those who have the power to approve and finance the important transportation projects which London so badly needs, to make the next fifty years as memorable as the first.

London Transport's collection of historic vehicles was first put on public display in the early 1960s at the Museum of British Transport in Clapham. When the museum closed in 1971, and most of the rail collection was transferred to the new National Railway Museum at York, a new home was found for the London Transport material at Syon Park, Brentford. In the late 1970s the opportunity arose to move the growing collection to a central London location in Covent Garden. The Victorian Flower Market was renovated and adapted to house a new and more comprehensive London Transport Museum, which was opened by HRH The Princess Anne in March 1980. The museum tells the story of nearly two centuries of public transport and its impact on the growth of London.

(1) An LGOC 'garden seat' horse bus of the 1880s (left) with its successor, the 'B' type motor bus introduced in 1910 (right).

(2) A section of the museum displays dealing with road transport in Victorian London.

(3) A former West Ham Corporation electric tramcar built in 1910 (right) with three LGOC motor buses of the inter-war period: a 'K' type (route 37) built in 1920, an 'NS' type (route 29) of 1927 and an 'ST' type (route 321) of 1931.

1

2

3

(4) Two of the museum's electric tramcars: the 1910 West Ham car (right) and a former London County Council 'E/1' class car of the same age (centre), which was in service for over 40 years.

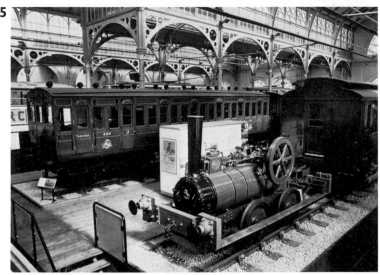

(5) Three of the rail exhibits: an 1899 Metropolitan Railway 'Bogie' stock coach (left), an Aveling & Porter steam locomotive of 1872 used on the Wotton Tramway in Buckinghamshire, which became the Metropolitan Railway's Brill Branch (centre) and a District Line 'Q23' stock driving motor car built in 1923 (right).

(6) Metropolitan Railway 'A' class steam locomotive No. 23, built in 1866, which remained in service with London Transport until 1948.

1

Three new garages and a large bus station were opened in 1981.

(1 & 2) A bus station was opened in May, at Harrow-on-the-Hill, providing convenient interchange between bus services and the Underground. It was the first on London Transport to have a fully enclosed waiting area with automatically opening doors, a public address system, and a tea bar.

(3) In April the first completely new central London bus garage for over 25 years was opened at Ash Grove, Hackney. It can house 170 vehicles and is equipped with the latest

2

3

maintenance, bus washing and staff facilities.

(4) In August a new garage for 110 buses was opened at Westbourne Park. The bed of the overhead M40 Westway was ingeniously incorporated in the design of the roof.

(5) In October the new Plumstead Garage was opened. This has space for 150 buses, and, like the other two garages, the most up-to-date engineering and staff facilities. In each case the opening of a new garage has enabled two outdated premises to be closed.

(6) The controversial, but well intentioned, 'Fares Fair' scheme, introduced on 4th October 1981 at the request of the GLC, reduced bus and Underground fares by an average of 33 per cent. Following legal action, the GLC was forced to abandon the scheme. Most London Transport fares were doubled in March 1982, but the popular concept of zonal fare structures, introduced with 'Fares Fair', was retained.

4

5

6

(1) Harlesden, Jubilee
Clock, 1936.

(2) South Harrow, 1932.

(3) Vauxhall Cross, 1936.

(4) Harlesden, Jubilee Clock, 1983.

(5) South Harrow, 1982.

(6) Vauxhall Cross, 1982.

London Transport has always promoted the advantages of public transport through stylish poster advertising, backed up with a comprehensive range of free maps and leaflets.

(1 & 2) Shopping by tube: posters by Frank Newbould 1934 (1) and Foote, Cone & Belding 1978 (2).

(3 & 4) Evening entertainment by tube: posters by A. Belding 1935 (3), and by Dewynters Ltd for the Society of West End Theatres, 1982 (4).

(5) The London Underground network, 1983.

(6) A selection of London Transport road and rail maps, 1933–1983.

1

A Cheap Day Tub saves getting th

Save up to a third with a Cheap Day Tube Return is 35p or more. After 1000 weekdays and a

2

THE LONDON UNDERGROUND

5

3

4

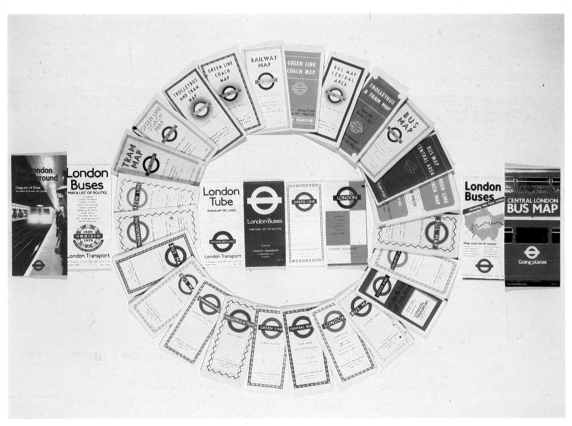

6

General

T. C. Barker and Michael Robbins—A History of London Transport Vol 2: The Twentieth Century to 1970 (Allen & Unwin 1976)

Christian Barman—The Man Who Built London Transport, A Biography of Frank Pick (David & Charles 1979)

John R. Day—A Source Book of London Transport (Ward Lock 1982)

Charles Graves—London Transport At War 1939–45 (LT 1978)

Michael Levey—London Transport Posters (LT 1976)

London Transport Annual Reports 1934 onwards

Buses

Barry Arnold and Mike Harris—Reshaping London's Buses (Ian Allan 1982)

Ken Blacker—RT, The Story of a London Bus (Capital Transport 1979)

J. Graeme Bruce and Colin H. Curtis—The London Motor Bus (LT 1977)

Colin H. Curtis—Buses of London (LT 1979)

Colin H. Curtis—The Routemaster Bus (Midas Books 1981)

John R. Day—The Story of the London Bus (LT 1973)

A. McCall—Green Line (New Cavendish Books 1980)

D. W. K. Jones and B. J. Davis—Green Line 1930–1980 (London Country Bus Services Ltd 1980)

George Robbins and Alan Thomas—London Buses Between The Wars (Marshall, Harris & Baldwin 1980)

Bob Scanlan—A Lifetime of London Bus Work (Transport Publishing Co. 1979)

Kenneth Warren—Fifty Years of the Green Line (Ian Allan 1980)

Trams and Trolleybuses

Ken Blacker—Trolleybus (Capital Transport 1978)

Terence Cooper (ed)—The Wheels Used To Talk To Us (Sheaf Publishing 1980)

John R. Day—London's Trams and Trolleybuses (LT 1977)

D. W. Willoughby and E. R. Oakley—London Transport Tramways Handbook (published by the authors 1972)

Underground

J. Graeme Bruce—Tube Trains Under London (LT 1977)

J. Graeme Bruce—Steam to Silver (Capital Transport 1983)

John R. Day—The Story of London's Underground (LT 1979)

John R. Day—The Story of the Victoria Line (LT 1969)

H. G. Follenfant—Reconstructing London's Underground (LT 1975)

Brian Hardy—LPTB Rolling Stock 1933–1948 (Bradford Barton 1981)

Chris Heaps—London Transport Railways Album (Ian Allan 1978)

H. F. Howson—London's Underground (Ian Allan 1981)

Alan A. Jackson and D. F. Croome—Rails Through The Clay (Allen & Unwin 1964)

Charles E. Lee—Booklets on the individual Underground lines (LT various dates)

Some of these books are now out of print, but reference copies may be consulted by appointment at the London Transport Museum Library, Covent Garden, London WC2E 7BB (Tel. 01 379 6344).